MINNEAPOLIS–ST. PAUL
THE CITIES, THEIR PEOPLE

by Robert T. Smith

photography by Steve Schneider

American Geographic Publishing
Helena, Montana

All rights reserved

William A. Cordingley, Chairman
Rick Graetz, Publisher
Mark Thompson, Director of Publications
Barbara Fifer, Assistant Book Editor

Robert T. Smith has written in and about Minneapolis-St. Paul for 32 years, working for the *Tribune* and the *Star Tribune* (at one time he was the youngest city editor of a major metropolitan daily). Smith was news editor of *Time* magazine's Washington bureau and deputy chief of its Paris bureau before returning to finish his news career in the cities. He continues to write a weekly column, some of which have been published in two volumes, for the *Star-Tribune*.

Steve Schneider, who holds a master's degree in photojournalism from the University of Minnesota, has been a Twin-Cities-area commercial photographer for nine years. He has numerous free-lance publication credits, and has contributed regularly to the Iron Range Communities Documentation Project.

Library of Congress Cataloging-in-Publication Data
Smith, Robert Tighe, 1926-
   Minneapolis-St. Paul : the cities, their people / by Robert T. Smith.
     p. cm. -- (Minnesota geographic series ; no.2)
   ISBN 0-938314-47-5 (pbk.) : $15.95
   1. Minneapolis (Minn.) -- Description. 2. Saint Paul (Minn.) -- Description. 3. Minneapolis (Minn.) -- History. 4. Saint Paul (Minn.) -- History.
I. Title. II. Series.
F614.M6S65 1988   88-10442
977.67'579 -- dc19   CIP

ISBN 0-938314-47-5
© 1988 American Geographic Publishing, P.O. Box 5630, Helena, MT 59604. (406) 443-2842.
Text © 1988 Robert T. Smith
Design by Len Visual Design; Linda Collins, graphic artist.
Printed in Hong Kong by Nordica International Ltd.

Front cover: *Winter Carnival fireworks, St. Paul.* STEVE SCHNEIDER
Back cover: *Loring Park, Minneapolis, in spring.* STEVE SCHNEIDER
Title page: *St. Paul buildings.* STEVE SCHNEIDER
Page 2, left: *Minneapolis' 7th Street.* ***Right:*** *Minneapolis at minus 30°.* STEVE SCHNEIDER PHOTOS
Left top: *Minnesota's State Capitol on a hill overlooking downtown St. Paul.* MICHAEL MAGNUSON
Left bottom: *The Minnesota Vikings battle the Washington Redskins in the Metrodome.* STEVE SCHNEIDER
Above: *A sunset complements Minnesota's State Capitol.* STEVE SCHNEIDER

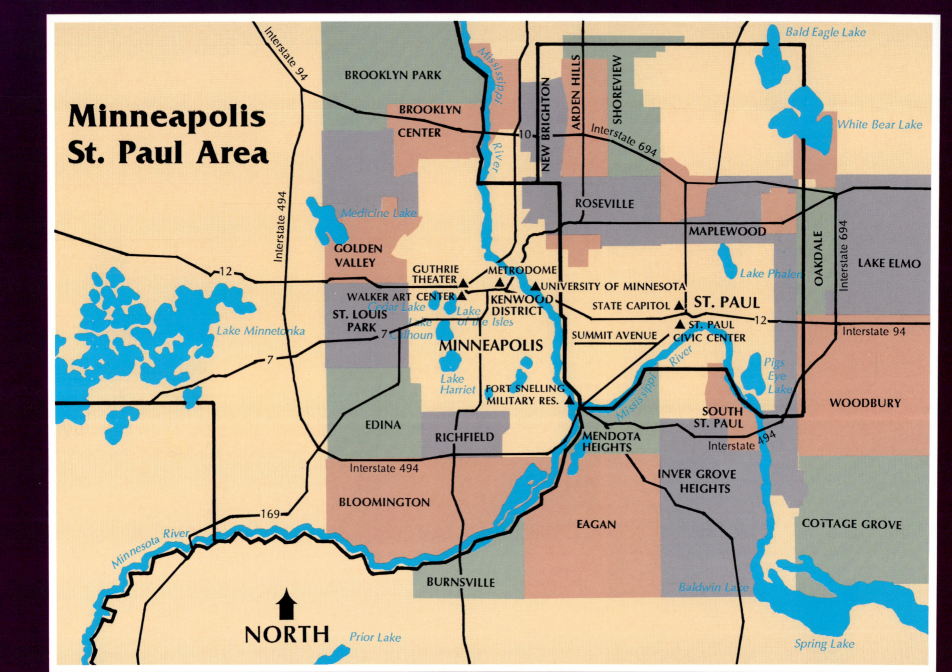

CONTENTS

Chapter 1
TWIN CITIES 6
Heckuva Deal

Chapter 2
LIFESTYLE 34
You Bet

Chapter 3
MINNEAPOLIS HISTORY 48

Chapter 4
ST. PAUL HISTORY 60

Chapter 5
TWIN CITIES ECONOMY 72

Chapter 6
POLITICS 88
No Insinuendoes, Please

FOR FURTHER READING 102

CHAPTER 1

THE TWIN CITIES
HECKUVA DEAL

Above: Snowmobiles go at it during a race that is part of the St. Paul Winter Carnival.
Right: A night view of the Minneapolis skyline. STEVE SCHNEIDER PHOTOS

They created the rock star, Prince, and nurtured the thoughtful singer-compser, Bob Dylan. They were haven at times for writers Sinclair Lewis and F. Scott Fitzgerald and they inspired some politicians to high national office. They were a springboard for actors and actresses: Eddie Albert, Arlene Dahl, Loni Anderson. They educated some exceptional journalists, including Eric Severeid, Harry Reasoner and Hedley Donovan. They are the Twin Cities.

In the early days, they attracted many bright, ambitious settlers who created a stable society as well as a stable economy. They kept the air pure and the noise down, except for airplanes, and they saw to it that a culture of theater, music and art was established—a culture far above the expectations of an area of not many more than 2 million people

They created a school system for the children that is responsible for one of the best-educated populations in the nation. They lured brilliant, creative business people to come and use their talents to build successful companies. And at the same time, they insisted that those people contribute to local society, both in time and money.

They established one of the most elaborate and capable medical communities, headed by the University of Minnesota, a pioneer in open-heart surgery. They preserved their lakes and parks and made sure there would be much open space in them. They also insisted that their people be open and friendly.

They expanded and built new, tall office buildings and fascinating places to shop. And they maintained their love of the outdoors. They are the Twin Cities.

The beauty of an autumn sunrise, and of the northern lights, a klieg-light sort of spectacle. The roar of snowmobiles running alongside suburban roads. The lineup of limousines at Northrop Auditorium, bringing people in formal clothes to attend the Metropolitan Opera.

The scene of the homeless, huddled under bridges over the Mississippi River. The white mushroom cloud that spills from the downtown Minneapolis steam-heat plant. The boom of the gun that starts sailboat races on the lakes in summer, and the cutting sound of skate blades on the lakes in winter.

The sound of "God Bless America," ringing from the carillon-bell tower of the City Hall in Minneapolis on the Fourth of July. The non-smell of clean air and the taste of good water.

The multicolored Christmas decorations, on trees and shrubs in residential neighborhoods—and the tiny white lights on the trees along the Nicollet Mall. The church bells every Sunday in both Minneapolis and St. Paul. The sight of the two watchdogs on the hills near downtown St. Paul the State Capitol and St. Paul Cathedral.

These are some of the things of the Twin Cities, a settlement that is diverse and complicated and fascinating.

St. Paul's Town Square Park, a mixture of stark and quaint.
STEVE SCHNEIDER

The Weather

The Twin Cities metropolitan area truly has four seasons. It gets hot in the summer: temperatures above 100° are not uncommon. The area is nationally known for its winters: 20° to 30° below zero is not uncommon.

The lowest temperature in Twin Cities modern record-keeping history was 34° below in January of both 1936 and 1970. But the *Pioneer* records show a low of minus 41° on Jan. 21, 1888. In July of 1936, the hottest temperature was recorded: 108°. The *Pioneer* records, which some dispute, show no higher temperature.

Spring is moderate and fresh and rejuvenating. And autumn is cool and filled with beautiful multicolored leaves.

The Twin Cities are at about the same latitude as Rome, Italy. But the similarity, in terms of weather, ends there.

As to storms, the region has experienced about everything except hurricanes and typhoons. The cities are on the northern ridge of the region that gets the most tornadoes in the nation.

Two of the 10 worst Minnesota tornadoes, for instance, struck the Twin Cities. On August 20, 1904, 15 people were killed in a Twin Cities tornado. Sixteen were killed on May 6, 1965, when a funnel cloud touched down in the area.

Severe thunderstorms occur on occasion. One of the worst happened July 23-24, 1987, during which more than 19" of rain fell. Tornadoes struck at the same time, leveling a dozen homes. Damage was estimated between $40 and $50 million. It was called "The Rainfall of the Century."

The most devastating blizzard hit the Twin Cities—and much of the state—on Armistice Day, November 11, 1940. It unexpectedly dumped 16.8" of blowing snow on the Twin Cities. Statewide, 59 people died in that storm.

To make the winter, at below-zero temperatures, more livable, there are the skyways in both Minneapolis and St. Paul. They are second-story "tunnels" that connect downtown buildings. They make it possible for people to walk warm and comfortable through the downtown areas.

Some springs, when there is a heavy snowmelt combined with heavy rains, the cities are flooded along the Mississippi and Minnesota rivers. There have been springtimes when houses have floated down a river and cars were completely covered by flood waters.

On rare occasions, the Twin Cities weather gets goofy. The winter of 1986-1987, for instance, was extremely mild. Meteorologist Bruce Watson calls it "the year without winter."

There were only 17" of snow all that winter. Often, that much snow falls in a week in the Twin Cities. That winter of 1986-1987 also was warm, with no temperatures below freezing until November 1. And the lowest temperature for the season was 14° below. Reports Watson in the *Minnesota Weatherguide Calendar:*

"For a combination of warmth and lack of snowfall, it was unsurpassed in the past 168 years. Only the season of 1877-78 was warmer, and not by much. However this season had much less snow.

"There is a third part to this story. Not only was snow scarce, but so was rain long before and after the snow season! One of the greatest dry periods in local weather history began on Oct. 13, 1986."

Aside from the occasional severe or freak weather, the Twin Cities normally enjoy the benefits of an area of four seasons.

The Twin Cities metropolitan area enjoys the benefits of an area that has four seasons.

This page: *Autumn in Minneapolis—a most colorful time of the year.*
Facing page: *The 1940 Armistice Day Blizzard brought death and paralyzed the Twin Cities.*
MINNESOTA HISTORICAL SOCIETY

Some action at the Blade Run, a Lake Harriet winter event to raise funds for the American Lung Association of Hennepin County.

Facing page: *The Mississippi River shortly before dawn.*
STEVE SCHNEIDER PHOTOS

The Lakes

New York City has its sky-reaching buildings. Washington, D.C., has it monuments. Philadelphia has its history. And Minneapolis has its lakes. The inner-city Minneapolis lakes are not just ornamental. They are regularly used by the people.

The Indians fished in these lakes, but mostly left them untouched. Then along came Zebulon Pike, the famed explorer. For 60 gallons of liquor and $4,000 in 1805, the Indians sold Pike all the Minneapolis lakes, and adjacent land, most of St. Paul and the land where the Mississippi and Minnesota rivers come together.

In 1884, Gideon Pond, a Congregational minister, built the first Minneapolis home. He located it on Lake Calhoun. It was a quiet, peaceful place to live, and soon more people migrated to the lakes—to get away from the hubbub of the downtown area.

By the late 1880s, resort hotels lined the shores of Calhoun and, with foresight, the city fathers decided the lakes belonged to everyone. Although opposed by some citizens, the leaders got the approval of the majority. There followed a massive restoration project that eliminated the swamps and unwanted growth surrounding the lakes.

The result: Minneapolis has some of the most beautiful inner-city lakes in the world, and one huge lake to the west. Here are some of the major ones, including one lake east of St. Paul:

Lake Minnetonka

The largest body of water in the Twin Cities area is Lake Minnetonka, west of Minneapolis. Its shoreline runs for about 91 miles.

Actually, Minnetonka is a series of lakes and bays, with names such as Priest's, Maxwell, Smithtown, North Arm. The bays once were separate little lakes, but were connected by channels.

Boating, both motor and sailing, is big business on the lake. On summer weekends, hundreds of boats cruise the waters, often forced to run slowly bow to stern.

In the late 1880s, the very wealthy had summer homes on Minnetonka. As Author Virginia Brainard Kunz put it:

"For most of the families, it was a big production. They moved out their linen and their china. They'd take their cow"

Later, the wealthy constructed year-round mansions in which descendants of the families, such as the Pillsburys and Heffelfingers, still live.

Sailing was the major sport of the wealthy, many of whom were from New England and had learned to sail on the Atlantic. Minnetonka was considered one of the most popular resorts in the country.

In those days, a big attraction was the *streetcar* boats. For 10 cents, you could ride a trolley from the Twin Cities to the lake, then board a boat designed in the shape of a streetcar. A brochure described the ride:

"The boats pass beautiful islands, handsome cottage colonies, picturesque channels, beautiful bays and charming vistas of blue dancing water everywhere."

Since 1911, Minnetonka has been stocked with fish. The first dumping was 20 cans of lake trout. Since then, millions of fish have been planted: bass, walleyes, north-

ern pike. The bays offer an assortment of panfish, including crappies and sunfish.

In recent time, Minnetonka has been the lake of all people. It now has homes ranging from the mansions of old to shacks.

Lake Calhoun

Lake Calhoun has 3.12 miles of shoreline, covers 421.3 acres, is 90″ deep and contains 4,835 million gallons of water. It first was named Lake of the Loons *(Mde Med'oza)* by the Indians, but later became Lake Calhoun as a salute to John Caldwell Calhoun, Secretary of War in President James Monroe's cabinet. It was Calhoun who established Fort Snelling.

One of the first controversies involving the lake occurred in 1890. Some swimmers complained of having to travel to and from their lake in their bathing suits. There was no place to change at the lake.

In those days, modesty had a high place in society. To appease these swimmers, the city built a bathhouse on the east shore of Calhoun—for men only. In probably one of the first feminist outcries in Minnesota, women objected strongly to such discrimination. They won, and eventually got their own bathhouse.

The lake is bounded by trees of many species: oak, elm, willow, cottonwood, maple, spruce. People often plant a tree near the lakes in memory of a deceased friend or relative.

On a hill on the east shore is St. Mary's Greek Orthodox Church, an edifice with a golden dome that, on sunny days, shimmers over the lake.

Lake Calhoun once was a place for fruit. Steven Kaplan, in a *Minneapolis Star Tribune Sunday Magazine* article, quotes a pioneer homesteader:

"In many places the trees were literally impurpled by the masses of grapes; plums and cherries were equally abundant and, of berries, especially strawberries, there was no end. On the north shore of Calhoun, there was a bed of the latter of more than an acre in extent, in which one could hardly set foot without crushing the berries. Wagonloads of people used to resort there, and return laden with bushels of the luscious fruit."

The lake is a sanctuary for wild birds, including Canada geese, ducks and coots. Some stay until the open water gives way to ice—a much longer time than their cousins in other parts of the state.

Today, Calhoun is much less commercial than it was in the late 1880s. Then there were resorts and hotels on the lake, and much more of a carnival atmosphere. But that era ended when the star inn, the Hotel Lyndale, burned down in 1888. Lake Minnetonka, the largest lake in the Twin Cities area, took over as a resort haven.

The cost of living around the lake is high: mansions can sell for hundreds of thousands. But rarely is a house around the lake on the market long.

Calhoun is a high-class lake, but there is another more elite: Lake of the Isles.

Lake of the Isles

Unlike many Twin Cities lakes, Isles is not oval. It twists and turns like a country road. It is smaller than Calhoun (only 107 acres) and shallower (54″ maximum), yet has its own interest and charm. Isles is easily more intimate.

Some of the wealthiest people of the Twin Cities live along Isles. Back in 1913, Charles Gates, scion of a family made rich in commodities and steel, built an Isles home for more than $1 million. Gates died before he could move in and the man who bought it never moved in. After *his*

Above: *Windsurfing is not for the weak in spirit. It's becoming a more common sight on Lake Harriet in Minneapolis.*
Left: *Lake of the Isles in Minneapolis—a healthful walk.*

Facing page: *A lonely guitarist serenades a sunset at Lake Calhoun in Minneapolis.* STEVE SCHNEIDER PHOTOS

A calm scene on Lake Harriet in Minneapolis, with the skyline in the background. STEVE SCHNEIDER

Facing page: *A favorite summertime adventure: aboard a paddleboat on the St. Croix River, near St. Paul.* MICHAEL MAGNUSON

death, the never-lived-in million-dollar house was destroyed.

Isles was named after its islands. In its early history, Isles had four islands: two called the Maples, Mike's Island and Raspberry. The Maples were victims of progress: the Chicago, Milwaukee and St. Paul Railway, in the process of building tracks, turned the Maples into hills. Now, only Mike's and Raspberry remain.

If real estate operators had had their way, the islands today would be neighborhoods of the wealthy. But the island land was acquired by the city and turned into a home for wildlife, including waterfowl. Inhabiting the islands now are majestic black-crown night herons, American egrets, screech owls, Canada geese and wood ducks, among other birds. The herons nest high on treetops and people make special trips at dawn or dusk to watch the graceful herons leave or return to their nests.

Isles, in the 1880s, gave birth to the Kenwood district. It was developed near the lake, but on higher ground. The lake then was insect-ridden and had a marshy perimeter. But, in their nearby homes above the lake, Kenwoodians could view their lake without the problems.

A colorful bit of Lake Isles history involves horse racing on ice. It began in 1897 and continued until 1929, and featured race horses pulling sulkies on the lake's frozen surface. Thousands lined the south shore to witness the sport.

In modern times, Isles has been a scene of natural beauty, a place to go for those who seek serenity and want to hide from the bustle of city life.

Perhaps the most famous filming of Isles was part of the beginning of television's "Mary Tyler Moore Show," its star pictured striding athletically along the Isles shore.

Lake Harriet

It's a family lake, a place to picnic or hear a concert, as well as take part in lake sports. Lake Harriet, hidden by trees, is a scene of children frolicking within sight of parents, of an elderly couple listening to a local orchestra playing "Meet Me in St. Louis." It's a place where teenagers stroll along beaches or honk at each other from their used cars on the lakeside drive.

A main part of the Harriet is its pavilion, a grey-blue structure with huge windows overlooking the lake. It is the fourth pavilion in the lake's history.

In 1889, Twin City Rapid Transit Co. established a trolley line to Harriet. To promote the line, the trolley firm built a pavilion on the lake. It was thought that a burlesque show might draw crowds. It did: crowds of angry family-oriented people and some city officials. Out went burlesque and in came opera and band concerts.

But this pavilion was too small to handle the increasing number of people who frequented the lake, and a second showplace was constructed in 1891. This one sported a cafeteria and a floating bandstand. As happened to so many early lakeside buildings, the pavilion burn down 12 years later.

The third pavilion was a victim of severe weather. It was fancier than the second one, with two long wings, one supporting a roof garden. Concerts were held on that roof. In 1925, a tornado swept the area and turned the pavilion into a pile of kindling. For more than 60 years, a small wooden bandstand with nothing special about it served Lake Harriet visitors.

A footnote to Harriet's history: in 1899, Myrtle Brown and Benjamin May made the front pages of Minneapolis newspapers. They got married in an electric launch on the lake.

As with Calhoun and Isles, Harriet is lined with elegant, spacious, expensive homes. Unlike Calhoun, there are no commercial buildings at Harriet except a refreshment stand run by the Park Board.

Harriet was named after Harriet Lovejoy Leavenworth, wife of Col. Henry Leavenworth, first commander at Fort Snelling.

White Bear Lake

There is a legend about White Bear Lake, east of St. Paul, perpetuated by Mark Twain in his book, *Life on the Mississippi*.

It seems there was an Indian, a Dakota Sioux warrior, considered a coward by his chief.

He, naturally, fell in love with the chief's daughter and was rejected for marriage by her father.

Under the branches of a huge elm tree on White Bear Lake's Manitou Island, the warrior met secretly with the chief's daughter. A white bear made his way slowly across the frozen lake and attacked.

The bear grabbed the daughter, but the warrior rose to the occasion and slew the bear with his knife. There was the happy ending: the young couple were married and their children frolicked on the bear's tanned skin.

Or, there is a second version. The warrior dies in the fight with the bear. So does the bear. And their spirits even today are wandering the lake in search of each other.

In any case, there never has been a sighting of either the bear or the warrior by residents of White Bear Lake, the St. Paul area's answer to Lake Minnetonka west of Minneapolis.

White Bear covers 2,368 acres and has a maximum depth of 82'. Its average depth is 20' and one third of the lake is only 15' deep. The shoreline is mostly sandy beach.

The fish range from walleyes and bluegills to bullheads and carp. The lake boasts the posh White Bear Yacht Club.

As with Lake Minnetonka, sailboat races and just plain sailing are prominent parts of White Bear use. But there are swimming and, of course, fishing, too.

Above: *St. Paul's Como Zoo takes on a Christmas atmosphere.*
Right: *A table-sitting cat in the south Minneapolis house.*

Facing page: *Minnehaha Falls: scene of weddings and suicides.*
STEVE SCHNEIDER PHOTOS

The most exclusive section is boot-shaped Manitou Island, where some of St. Paul's wealthiest families have built summer cottages since the 1880s. As of 1987, there were 27 houses on the island, most of them valued at more than $350,000.

Some 130 years ago, the lake area was one of wild forests, that included white oak, tamarac, sugar maples and black burr.

According to author Nancy L. Woolworth, the first real estate boom in White Bear Lake took place during the summer of 1850. Wrote Woolworth:

"But no real settlement was begun until 1851 when interest in farming the area was aroused by James M. Goodhue's *Minnesota Pioneer*…Goodhue began writing enticing descriptions of the land north of St. Paul, making it sound most appealing to farmers…."

Those who did come to the area were entranced by the lake itself, which, even then, was a beautiful expanse of water and island surrounded by forests.

Today, with its adjacent town also called White Bear Lake, the lake stands as one of the most famous in Minnesota.

Said one resident of Manitou Island, Dolores Westin: "When we cross the bridge to the island it still feels as if we're going to paradise. There are so many times I say, 'Isn't this beautiful?' You'd think I'd get tired of saying that after 30 years."

Kenwood

In the 1870s, some of the wealthy people of Minneapolis moved to an area east of Lake of the Isles, but close to downtown. They established Kenwood.

It became a neighborhood of mansions and huge lawns and streets lined with birch, oak and maple trees, among others. On some avenues, the tall trees touch at the top, forming their versions of cathedrals.

For decades, Kenwood remained the neighborhood of the rich. Many of the mansions were named after the first owners, and still carry those names.

It was the early practice of many Kenwood residents to build summer homes on Lake Minnetonka, west of Minneapolis. But when the automobile arrived, the residents winterized their Lake Minnetonka homes and moved there. Cars, they believed, had made Kenwood less exclusive.

Dan Cohen, lawyer and Minneapolis politician who lived in Kenwood for 13 years beginning in 1966, describes the neighborhood:

"Kenwood is a place where I could almost always panhandle a ride to work in the morning at the bus stop, or, if I couldn't, take comfort in sharking a ride downtown with a battalion of local business conquerors.

"Riding a bus is *in*. You could see that kind of reverse snobbery in other ways, too. Lawns are mowed, not manicured. A certain genteel seediness prevails.

"Yet, you won't find another place in the city where two candidates for alderman in the last election seem to have been able to finance their own campaigns and nobody much cared; and where there are fewer basketball hoops on garages, but more Volvos and Mercedeses inside them."

In recent time, Kenwood has changed some. The older residents died off, and a younger, yuppier population settle in. This post World War II generation wasn't wealthy, but they were mainly college-educated, very urban and affluent.

In 1980, tongue firmly implanted in cheek, the late columnist, Don Morrison, then of the *Minneapolis Star,* explained:

"Vertiginous real estate prices in recent years may seem to support the notion that the area is a bastion of pampered wealth. Not so many years ago, however, it provided large and laughably inexpensive houses in which

17

the unpampered postwar masses could stash their laughably large baby boom families.

"Even newspaper people lived there—and no neighborhood harboring such Dogpatch squatters can get away with class pretensions."

There are no specific boundaries of Kenwood, but it is generally accepted that Walker Art Center and the Guthrie Theater are part of the neighborhood.

And there are those who think Kenwood today is more a state of mind than a neighborhood.

Minnehaha Creek

Meandering through south Minneapolis is a creek that roars like a mountain stream at some points or slips slowly through quiet pools shaded by overhanging weeping willows.

The 22-mile Minnehaha Creek flows from Lake Minnetonka, through western Minneapolis suburbs and into the city. It frolics over Minnehaha Falls and ends up in the Mississippi River.

In the summer, the creek is a challenge for canoeists and in winter the Hans Brinkers come out to skate for miles on it.

There is danger for the inexperienced canoeists, particularly involving the falls. You must take your canoe out or it could be disaster. Ralph Thornton of the *Minneapolis Star-Tribune* reports the scene at a tenth of a mile before the creek dives into the Mississippi:

"Last chance to take out before Minnehaha Falls. Those missing this takeout may notice a one-foot-square sign in the trees on the south bank by the last bridge, near the Minnehaha Falls refectory, stating: 'Danger—Falls 20 Feet Ahead.'

"When you see the sign, it may be too late. When you see the statue of Hiawatha, it *is* too late."

Minnehaha Falls

Where the falls of Minnehaha
Flash and gleam among the oak trees
Laugh and leap into the valley.
—Longfellow: "Song of Hiawatha"

Small by Niagara standards, the 40′ Minnehaha Falls makes up for its smallness in a quieter beauty. Located near the end of Minnehaha Creek, the falls spill out of a wooded area and slap the creek bed below.

Before 1889, the falls were nestled in a wildly gorgeous area. Creation of Minnehaha Park tamed that beauty. To make way for the park, trees were cut down and buildings went up. At one point, 10,000 school children were persuaded to take hold of cables and tow the house of John Stevens, a Minnesota pioneer, from what was then Minneapolis to the park, where it remains today.

Yearly, thousands of people, tourists and locals, visit the falls. Couples have been married there and it has been the scene of suicides.

Basilica of St. Mary

People from throughout the United States come to Minneapolis to visit the majestic Basilica of St. Mary. The cathedral stands on a hill near Loring Park and its copper dome can be seen for miles.

Rivaling the cathedrals of Europe, the basilica is the main symbol of the Roman Catholic church in the city.

The congregation was formed more than 100 years ago, but the building—a modern Renaissance combination of Gothic, Romanesque and Byzantine architecture—wasn't completed until 1914.

The interior, with its arches and large stained-glass windows, is awesome. Said one of the basilica's pastors, the Rev. Alfred Wagner: "When people first see it, their heads fall back and their mouths gape."

The Mississippi

It's a river all-important in the history of both Minneapolis and St. Paul. Its St. Anthony Falls created the mills that created Minneapolis, and its boat traffic was essential to the establishment of St. Paul.

"Old Man River," which begins in Lake Itasca, Minnesota, is as fickle as a debutante at her debut. It can rise in anger, many feet above flood stage, and dump its waters on the homes and cars of those who dare to live on these banks.

Or, it can almost dry up, making river traffic difficult if not impossible. In the winter, it can freeze up, stopping all traffic.

It can be beautiful and it can be ugly, but always for the Twin Cities, he is important.

It is economical. By 1985 figures, the Mississippi carried about half the nation's grain exports—1.5 billion bush-

The Mississippi River is as fickle as a debutante at her debut.

Facing page: *The Minneapolis skyline from under the Tenth Avenue Bridge, one of many spanning the Mississippi River in the Twin Cities.*
STEVE SCHNEIDER

els—on the river barges. It did so for 0.7 cents a bushel, compared with 10 cents by truck and 2.6 cents by rail.

And, in the warmer months, the river is the playground of sailboaters and motorboaters in the Twin Cities, as well as those who love the leisurely paddleboat cruises.

In the winter, the river has been the home of the *Mississippi River Sculptor,* artists who camp under the Third Avenue Bridge in Minneapolis. They live there and they create there.

The river has inspired quaint projects along its banks: Riverplace, St. Anthony Main, Nicollet Island Park. These include restaurants, boutiques and other business establishments—mostly created with history in mind.

St. Paul's downtown sits just above the Mississippi. Since 1888, the river and its banks, with bluffs and woodlands nearby, have been protected by incorporation into the city park system.

St. Paul, born because of the Mississippi, wanted to better its relationship with "Old Man River."

Downtown Minneapolis

They are a block apart—Hennepin Avenue and the Nicollet Mall—but they are leagues apart in character.

Hennepin once was the Great White Way of Minneapolis. It was the avenue where families went for entertainment, for the legitimate theater or movies, for good restaurants and sensible shopping. There was no fear on Hennepin Avenue.

Today, it is dominated by adult book stores, noisy bars, cheap hotels and sometimes-dangerous street people. At night, it is not difficult to get robbed or mugged or both. Hennepin is a street of young runaways, tough troublemakers, prostitutes and lost souls.

Then there's the stylish Nicollet Mall, a street of department stores, shopping centers, specialty shops, restaurants and sidewalk cafes. It's as if a huge glass wall separated the two streets.

The Mall, center of downtown shopping, was designed for the pedestrian. At its dedication in 1967, landscape architect Lawrence Halprin called Nicollet Mall "the first in the world" to be devoted to walking people instead of the automobile. It is a meandering street, lined with trees and fountains and benches and sculpture. The curving avenue recalls the charm of medieval streets.

Among the major attractions on the Mall are the IDS Center, City Center and the Conservatory.

The IDS Center

For 43 years, the king of the Minneapolis skyline was the Foshay Tower. Now it is the runt.

When it opened in 1929, thousands gathered to dedicate the 32-story building, modeled after the Washington Monument. George Washington was the hero of Wilbur Foshay, whose money built the structure.

John Philip Sousa and his 75-piece band played for the dedication and Minneapolis had its centerpiece.

People identified regularly with the tower. For instance, a news photographer from Canada, who often got lost on assignment, would climb atop his car and look for the tower. Then he would head in that direction. When one had been out of town for a length of time, the tower often would be the first sight of home.

But the Foshay era ended in 1972, when the IDS (Investors Diversified) Center opened. Its 57 stories dwarfed Foshay and IDS became the king of the Minneapolis skyline. It still is.

On a clear day, the IDS tower, as it's commonly called, seems to blend in with the sky, giving it a floating effect. The "merging" with the sky occurs because of 42,614 panes of reflective glass that make up much of the building's outside surface.

The octagonal, $140-million structure required 373,000 man-hours to build, and contains 43 elevators and 1,285,000 square feet of space.

On the ground floor is the Crystal Court, from which you can see the sky through a slanted, glass, triangular roof-canopy.

In the center of the court is an indoor "outdoor" cafe, Au Bon Pain, with its red umbrellas over red tables by red chairs. On the sides of the court are stores and boutiques, ranging from Brooks Brothers to Scarlet Letters, a small stationery and gift shop.

There's room for 8,000 people in the center, and 3,000 can get a meal in its restaurants at the same time.

Since IDS, several buildings have been erected—all higher than the Foshay. Now, the Foshay is huddled 225′ below the IDS.

City Center

On its opening day in 1983, an estimated 100,000 people visited the City Center, a three-story retail complex claimed to be the inner-city answer to suburban malls. Guards were posted at the escalators to control traffic and prevent overloads.

Within a year, 90 percent of its 181,572 square feet of space was rented by 77 tenants. Stores range from apparel shops to those for home furnishings, to the European Flower Market. Great Expectations is a fine jewelry store, Corporate Woman and Victoria's Secret, apparel stores, and, among the restaurants, Grandma Gebhard's. There are specialty stores that feature books, records, luggage and shoes.

Over one entrance to the $250 million City Center is an 8′-long clear glass canopy, complete with multicolored banners. It juts eight feet over the sidewalk.

A pedestrian bridge allows University of Minnesota students to avoid busy Washington Avenue.

Facing page: *Christmas decorations at City Center in downtown Minneapolis.* STEVE SCHNEIDER PHOTOS

21

The Conservatory

Designed to bring high-priced shopping to downtown Minneapolis, the Conservatory opened in the fall of 1987. It is a glass-enclosed retail center on the south end of the Mall.

Designers used mainly natural materials, such as slate, birch, oak and marble, and soft shades of pink, ivory and mauve. Elevator interiors in the five-story building have marble tile walls and Oriental carpeting. But, most of all, the Conservatory is a series of small, but expensive and/or unusual stores.

At F.A.O. Schwarz, for instance, you can get a tiger-sized stuffed tiger for $950, a child-sized mink coat for $2,500, a mink bear for $5,000 or, for the kid who has everything, a birthday party for 14 in New York City for $14,000.

At St. Moritz Chocolatier, you might want a chocolate *Newsweek* cover ($20) or, for $300, a die of your corporate logo from which you can stamp out chocolate logos.

The Sharper Image offers "boy toys," including a radio-controlled hot-air balloon at $299, a battery-powered Porsche convertible at $199 and, for $1,595, a "getaway reclining chair" with a vibrating seat and stereo headset.

The $75 million Conservatory isn't for everybody, but even those with money have to have someplace to shop.

The Warehouse District

Minneapolis has put life into its old downtown warehouse district. Where once was the area of loading docks and noisy trucks, now is a neighborhood of more than 20 restaurants and bars with names such as Raleigh's and Bunkers and Cafe d'el Arte.

It is a district of art galleries and small specialty shops. The Wyman Building alone houses nine art galleries. The turn-of-the-century brick buildings, once blackened with soot, have been renovated and still sport their artistic cornices and filigrees.

Men in overalls have been replaced with well-dressed people. In a *Minneapolis Star Tribune* article, Jim Fuller wrote:

"Yet there are people on the sidewalks, especially during the day, and a surprisingly high percentage of them are dressed for business. Many of those in casual clothing are wearing designer jeans and smart jackets....The parking spaces in the area are jammed with the cars of the middle class—Hondas and Audis and Pontiacs and an occasional Mercedes or Corvette.

"Most surprising is the rapid coming and going from doorways beneath signs that call attention to restaurants and bars. At noon and after work, you'll find the numerous restaurants jammed with people in their upper 20s to mid 50s, dressed in pinstripes or fashionable leisure wear.

"The district now has some characteristics in common with famous and expensive redeveloped areas in bigger cities, such as New York's Soho or Chicago's Old Town."

Old Main Street vacant buildings were transformed into a shopping and restaurant area—with an eye toward preserving the charm of the past.

Facing page: *The Foshay Tower (center, with antenna on top) once was the tallest building in downtown Minneapolis.* STEVE SCHNEIDER PHOTOS

The Metrodome in downtown Minneapolis houses everything from sports events to rock concerts.

Facing page: *Landmark Center, in downtown St. Paul, formerly was the Federal Courts Building. Now it is an art, education and history center.*
STEVE SCHNEIDER PHOTOS

The Metrodome

Southeast of the main part of downtown Minneapolis is the Hubert H. Humphrey Metrodome, a $62 million enclosed sports stadium that survived despite the initial groans of many baseball fans who thought playing their sport indoors was obscene.

The Dome looks like a giant gray mushroom. Its roof is made of strands of fiberglass, woven into a thin fabric weighing one pound per square inch. That is covered with two layers of fiberglass cloth cut into 106 panels. The dome is two layers of the fabric, separated by a pocket of air.

On the second level, surrounding the field, are enclosed suites, complete with in-house television, commercial television, comfortable seats, selections of hors d'oeuvres and a bar.

The Metrodome is known for crowd noise. Unlike in open stadiums, the yells and screams of the crowd go right down on the field—and stay there.

Named after Minnesota's most famous politician, the Dome seats 63,000 for the National Football League's Minnesota Vikings, and 55,200 for the Minnesota Twins' baseball. It opened in 1982 and was the place the Twins won the World Series in 1987.

According to the *Minneapolis Star Tribune,* here are some of the highlights and lowlights in the history of the Metrodome:

"Inflation: The Dome was raised on Oct. 2, 1981.

"First roof collapse: Forty-eight days later, Nov. 19, 1981. After a 10-inch snowstorm, a panel tore and the roof collapsed like a shaken pie in an oven. Construction officials had promised the Dome could withstand up to 30 inches of snow.

"First indoor baseball game in Minnesota: April 6, 1982. Twins lose to Seattle 11-7.

"Second roof collapse: Dec. 28, 1982. Melting snow tore a fiberglass panel in the roof, and once again the Puff deflated. Workers scrambled to get the stadium ready for a Vikings game six days later.

"Most terrifying roof tear: April 26, 1986, bottom of the eighth inning. Winds outside the Dome suddenly increased from 10 miles per hour to almost 80 mph in seconds. The blast altered the air pressure within the Dome. Some of the air inside the building escaped through dampers. Monitoring devices went haywire. One hundred plugs in the roof that keep water from seeping from outside burst; water fell on the field. Light standards shook. A portion of the roof tore in right-center field. The Dome sagged.

"Greatest moment: May 4, 1984, fourth inning. Oakland's Dave Kingman lofts a towering popup, and the $3^{1}/_{2}$-inch-in-diameter baseball went through a 7-inch hole in the roof. Kingman was awarded a roof-rule double. Said Twins second baseman Tim Teufel: 'It's like a triple play—something that you would tell to your grandchildren, about the ball that went up and never came back down....We were all standing around like it was "Candid Camera".'

"Most bitter critique: For a change, George Steinbrenner and Billy Martin saw eye-to-eye. On May 7, 1985, Yankees manager Martin unleashed the ultimate Dome diatribe after the Twins beat the Yankees 8-6—when four Twins runs could be attributed to balls being lost in the lights and the roof: "This park should be barred from baseball....You win on fly balls or lose on fly balls. That's not major league baseball, that's amateur Little League." A day later, owner Steinbrenner released a statement that read: "If I wanted my players to be ping pong players, I would send them to China to play the Chinese National Team'."

Downtown St. Paul

With its sometimes narrow and sometimes crooked streets, downtown St. Paul is more European-looking than Minneapolis. It has a more intimate nature.

Guarded by the Mississippi on the south and both the State Capitol and the Cathedral of St. Paul on the north, downtown St. Paul seems a safe haven for a city of its size.

The specialty shops are apt to be operated by friendly, warm people without a snip of snobbery. Even the bigger departments stores have clerks who appear to love their jobs.

As in Paris or London or Rome, some of the streets don't seem to know where they are going. They dart off at angles from main avenues and tend to form small triangular "parks."

In Minneapolis, most downtown streets have numbers. In St. Paul they have names: Wabasha, St. Peter, Cedar, Jackson, Kellogg Boulevard.

The St. Paul Civic Center, a gathering place for entertainment and conventions, hosts sports ranging from the Minnesota State High School Basketball tournament to professional wrestling. The circular center also offers concerts by such popular artists as Barry Manilow and Peter, Paul and Mary. And each year, the center houses the St. Paul International Institute's Festival of Nations, an occasion to honor St. Paul's ethnic heritage.

The center project began in the early 1970s in the basement of the prestigious Minnesota Club. Some businessmen gathered to discuss a civic center and, one of them, Harold Cummings, described the initial reaction:

"There was an awful silence. Nobody said a word. Everybody stuck his hands under his pants and held them there. Then we all went upstairs for a drink and lunch."

But the project survived and, for $12.8 million, the 15,000-seat center became a reality.

Three other major downtown projects succeeded in St. Paul: the World Trade Center, Landmark Center and Lowertown.

The World Trade Center

One of the more ambitious St. Paul downtown projects is the $120 million Minnesota World Trade Center, a standout 37-story tower. It opened in September 1987 with festivities attended by 20 foreign ambassadors.

It is not huge by downtown standards, but a stretch for the conservative-in-architecture Saintly City. The center is made of polished red granite on the outside, with brown reflective windows. The lobby is studded with flamed granite, stainless steel and gray reflective glass.

There are 465,000 square feet of office space and, from the offices, you can see the Mississippi River or the skyline of downtown Minneapolis. The project is part of St. Paul Center, a four-block complex that includes a domed atrium centered by a large fountain. Flowers and potted trees surround it all. There are major department stores and specialty shops.

The center's founders hope that it eventually will become deeply involved with the network of other world trade centers—which, in total, have more than 45,000 businesses as affiliates.

Before it opened, St. Paul's Mayor George Latimer put the center in perspective:

"Today, St. Paul, which was founded as a riverport, remains the largest riverport in the Upper Midwest, serving a hinterland that stretches between Chicago and Seattle. This is a role that will be greatly magnified when the World Trade Center opens. It will mark a return to a vision by Empire-builder James J. Hill almost 100 years ago when his rail lines reached the Pacific and he set out to establish trade with the Orient. Even Hill was not breaking new ground. During the earlier years of the nineteenth century, shipping of furs down the Mississippi toward Europe by the Hudson Bay Company already made St. Paul a world trade center."

Landmark Center

In the 1960s, the federal government started to abandon the Old Federal Courts Building in the heart of downtown St. Paul. The future of the marvelous structure was in grave doubt. The building has been scheduled for demolition.

It's a castle-like structure with turrets around the top of the main building and two majestic towers. The five-story building is an artistic example of neo-romanesque architecture. Completed in 1902 at a cost of $2.5 million, it was described as "a work of art in architecture."

Originally, Old Federal Courts contained a post office and a customs house besides the courthouse. Later, it became headquarters for all federal offices in the Upper Midwest.

But the federal government outgrew it, contending there was a need for more modern quarters.

To the rescue came two men: Frank Marzitelli, founder of the St. Paul/Ramsey Arts and Science Council, and Georgia DeCoster, chairman of the St. Paul City Planning Commission's Historical Sites Committee. They organized, under Mayor Tom Byrne, a mayor's committee to save the building. It included many of the movers and shakers in St. Paul, people in business, politics, architecture, philanthropy.

They succeeded, with the help of others, in getting the federal government to give title to the city, and later to Ramsey County—and they raised $13.5 million to renovate the structure and turn it into a 200,000-square-foot home for arts, history and education, called the Landmark Center.

Spring flowers are abundant at the St. Paul Conservatory.
MICHAEL MAGNUSON

Facing page: *The Mississippi River, shown at St. Paul, still is an important shipping waterway.*
STEVE SCHNEIDER

Above: *The Minneapolis Institute of Art is one of the most prestigious museums in the nation.*
Right: *An interior view of the Landmark Center in St. Paul. It was restored at a cost of $13.5 million.*

Facing page: *A view inside the Minnesota State Capitol in St. Paul. It was built of Minnesota granite and Georgian marble in Italian-Renaissance style.*
STEVE SCHNEIDER PHOTOS

It was a long way from a place where gangsters of the Prohibition days were tried to a place that headquarters institutions such as the Schubert Club, the Ramsey County Historical Society and the St. Paul Chamber Orchestra.

Author Virginia Brainard Kunz (in *St. Paul: a Modern Renaissance*) tells of the before-and-after of the old building, which she says resembles a European city hall:

"The interior had been hacked up with wallboard, the lofty ceilings lowered with false ceilings covered with acoustical tile, the marble lobbies, courtrooms, and stained-glass skylights painted 'government green.' The building's granite exterior was darkened by grime and adorned by a ramshackle shed that was a post office loading dock...

"Then the exterior was cleaned, and the intricacy of its stone carving and the beauty of its pink granite stood revealed."

The inside also was stripped of its ugliness and renovated into a structure of awesome beauty.

Today, the center also includes the Minnesota Museum of Art and Community Program in Arts and Sciences (COMPAS), the biggest community arts agency in Minnesota, which has developed projects ranging from Dialogue (sponsoring joint programs for teachers and writers), to Accessible Arts, a project to inspire writings by the elderly, the handicapped, the lonely, those in hospitals and others.

Lowertown

It surrounded Old Smith Park, near the Mississippi River: 14 blocks of warehouses and manufacturing plants built in the 19th century. Today, Lowertown is something else.

Before it was a warehouse district, Lowertown was a residential neighborhood, with ornate houses and hotels, merchants and small, friendly stores. It was a return to that 100-year-old scene that the redevelopers wanted.

The centerpiece of Lowertown is Union Depot, once one of the most important railroad stations in the nation. The stone and granite building, in its heyday, was host to 150 trains a day, but that era ended. No one, however, wanted Union destroyed. It was redeveloped into a place of restaurants, bars and offices.

Near the depot is the General Office Building, constructed in the late 1880s by railroad magnate James J. Hill. Even in its early days, the seven-story structure of red brick was a fascinating sight. It featured a cast-iron gate, cozy fireplaces, marble decorations and a courtyard where Hill kept his riding horse.

General Office is now Lowertown Lofts, a unique apartment complex for writers and artists, a sort of Greenwich Village of St. Paul. The 29-unit project is a cooperative with the inhabitants involved in ownership of their apartments. Lofts is one reason St. Paul gained the sixth annual City Livability award.

Lowertown's Lambert's Landing was the site where early settlers docked their boats to found the Saintly City. Later, thousands came to Lambert's to start new lives or merely to visit a wilderness. The landing still exists, and is the docking area for river excursion boats, including the famous *Delta Queen*.

Cass Gilbert, a well respected turn-of-the-century architect, was responsible for two Lowertown buildings: a macaroni factory and the Pioneer Building. The macaroni factory is now American House Apartments, single-housing units for low-income people. Pioneer, with its stained-glass skylights, was restored by First National Bank of St. Paul.

Lowertown was redeveloped with the help of a $10 million grant from the McKnight Foundation. The Lowertown Redevelopment Corporation was created, and later Control Data contributed another $10 million to build a Business and Technology Center.

The St. Paul Cathedral originally was a small log chapel on the banks of the Mississippi.

Facing page: *Flowers decorate the grounds of the Minnesota State Capitol.* STEVE SCHNEIDER PHOTOS

The idea was to transform Lowertown from a decaying warehouse district to a bustling, imaginative neighborhood of stores and apartments and other establishments—all carefully designed to keep the historical flavor of the district.

Nineteenth-century street lamps were erected throughout the neighborhood, along with new curbs and sidewalks. The old Farmer's Market, at 10th and Jackson streets since 1902, was razed to make room for the Embassy Suites Hotel.

That caused some grumbling among the farmers, but Embassy Suites kept in tune with the neighborhood. It built a 19th-century–style hotel, with huge windows opening to balconies, with a center courtyard and atrium, with shrubs and trees and murals that do not demand attention. If you didn't know the seven-story hotel was built in the early 1980s, you would guess it dated back to the first glory days of Lowertown.

Cathedral of St. Paul

Guarding St. Paul from atop a high hill, the Cathedral of St. Paul is one of the largest church buildings in North America. It is more than 300' high and can seat 4,000 people.

Inside, the gold, blue and ivory dome is rimmed with eight series of windows. They represent the celestial hierarchy in scripture: thrones, dominions, powers, seraphim and cherubim, virtues, principalities, archangels and angels.

The *principal-church* of the Archdiocese of St. Paul began as a small log chapel on the banks of the Mississippi. In 1841, the Rev. Lucien Galtier, who built the structure, dedicated it to St. Paul the Apostle.

A brick building was constructed in 1851, then a stone structure in 1858. Famed Archbishop John Ireland decided to build the present cathedral in 1904. Designed by French architect E.L. Masqueray, it was constructed of Minnesota granite. It wasn't totally finished until 50 years after it was begun.

A highlight of the cathedral is the Blessed Virgin chapel, one of four located in the structure. Its walls are of marble imported from near Carrara, Italy. The centerpiece on an altar is a statue of Mary and Jesus. Stained-glass windows—depicting the birth and death of Jesus—are on each side of the statue.

On the 80th anniversary of groundbreaking for the cathedral, bells were installed in the south tower. Until then, 1986, the cathedral had been silent. Now the five bronze bells are used regularly, and can be heard for miles.

From the front steps, there is a panoramic view of downtown St. Paul and environs. The cathedral and the nearby capitol are the majestic twin crowns of St. Paul.

Minnesota's State Capitol

It's a lofty, elegant building which, like the Cathedral of St. Paul, oversees downtown St. Paul's skyline. The home of the lawmakers of Minnesota is an impressive structure visited yearly by thousands—many of them schoolchildren.

The capitol is topped by a dome with a golden charioteer and his team of horses at its base. Modeled after St. Peter's Church in Rome, the dome gleams on sunny days.

The golden charioteer and his horses adorn the dome of the State Capitol.
STEVE SCHNEIDER

The charioteer carries a horn of plenty, stuffed with Minnesota products. Inside the rotunda are a 2,000-pound chandelier—a huge ball of Italian crystal beads—and four-paneled paintings by Edward Simmons.

Balconies in the rotunda are decorated Minnesota-style: with golden gophers and north stars. Other parts of the Italian-Renaissance–style capitol are decorated with wheat, ladyslippers and corn, as well as gophers and stars.

The capitol exterior is constructed of Minnesota granite and white Georgian marble. The interior contains limestone and marble from Africa, Europe and the United States.

The Capitol's designer, Cass Gilbert, gained national fame because of his St. Paul creation. Gilbert, a St. Paul native, also directed the construction. The cost of the capitol, which was completed in 1904, was $4.5 million. In today's terms, that's about $200 million.

It is the third capitol for Minnesota. The first, built on the block bordered by 10th and Exchange streets and Wabasha and Cedar avenues, burned down in 1881. A second capitol, on the same property, became too small as Minnesota grew.

Summit Avenue

It's in the Crocus Hill neighborhood where F. Scott Fitzgerald and Sinclair Lewis once lived. The Minnesota governor's mansion is on it.

St. Paul's Summit Avenue, a wide, elm-lined thoroughfare, is considered one of the most elegant Victorian ways in the United States. It sweeps about five miles from the Mississippi River to the St. Paul Cathedral and remains the avenue of some of St. Paul's wealthiest and oldest families.

On Summit Avenue, James J. Hill, the railroad magnate, built a red sandstone mansion that was completed in 1891. The 32-room house, of Richardsonian Romanesque architecture, has a dining room that can accommodate 40 people. Today, Hill's mansion is a tourist attraction.

At 599 Summit, a row house, Fitzgerald finished *This Side of Paradise,* the novel that was to begin his fame. His relationship to Summit is described in the book *Landmarks—Old and New: Minneapolis and St. Paul and Surrounding Areas* by Lael Berman:

"While he [Fitzgerald] referred to stately Summit as 'a museum of American architectural failures,' the street was nonetheless the symbol of status and wealth, which seemed to elude his family.

"In recent years the row of eight rough-faced brownstone attached dwellings at 587-601 Summit, now called Summit Terrace, have become coveted addresses. Built in 1889, the townhouse-like structures with their myriad gables, turrets, and recessed doorways, are privately owned and/or rented as apartments and condominiums…"

The College of St. Thomas and Macalester College are on Summit, along with several churches. Some young professionals have moved into old mansions on Summit and others have built new houses. Explains author Carol Estocko in *Guest Informant—Fiftieth Anniversary Issue:*

"A number of new homes, architecturally compatible with the older ones, have popped up on the avenue in recent years. Though the face of Summit Avenue may be changing, the new appears to exist in harmony with the old, adding welcome vitality to the capital city without disturbing its rich, historic past."

The Twin Cities: a plains-state metropolitan complex, which has many hills and streets that run like mild rollercoasters. These are cities with much open space and parks and lakes and buildings with a history. They are cities of landscape, preserved through the decades by people who believed in nature. So who are these people and what do they do?

Downtown St. Paul—the historic St. Paul Hotel (left) and the modern Amhoist Building. STEVE SCHNEIDER

33

CHAPTER
2

LIFESTYLE
YOU BET

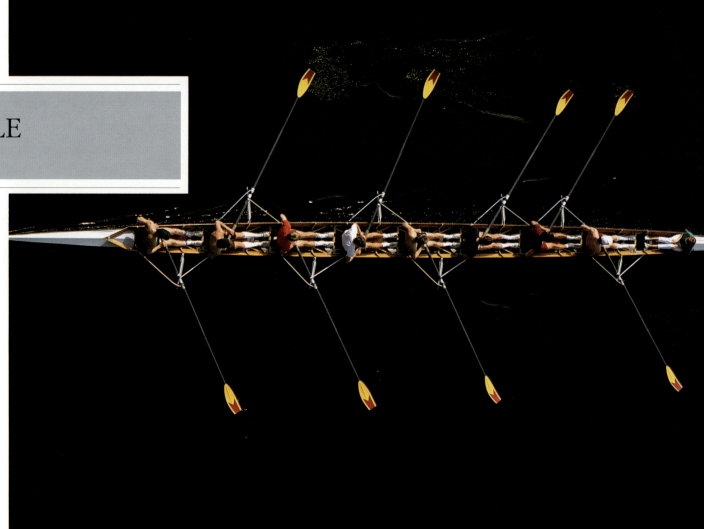

Above: *A quiet place for University of Minnesota students to study: Wilson Library on campus.*
Right: *A University of Minnesota crew on the Mississippi River.*

Facing page: *Minneapolis City Firemen battle a house fire.*
STEVE SCHNEIDER PHOTOS

There was a time, say 40 years ago, when you could characterize Twin Citians with some accuracy. They were hardworking people with a conservative lifestyle. They were mostly church-going folks who loved the outdoors. They were family oriented and thought New York City was sinful.

There were no adult book stores and an amiable little movie, *The Moon Is Blue,* was banned in St. Paul and barely tolerated in Minneapolis because it had words such as "virgin" in it.

Twin Citians preferred *Snow White and the Seven Dwarfs* and musicals rather than heavy Tennessee Williams fare. They wanted to be lightly entertained, not depressed by problems.

They read clean novels such as *How Green Was My Valley* and were disturbed when Clark Gable said "damn" in *Gone With the Wind*. They drank moderately for the most part, and thought drugs were something you got at a pharmacy.

They liked prayers in schools and felt that sex education belonged in the home, but rarely talked to their children about sex. They didn't do the stork story, but almost. Girls were expected to be virgins until they married and getting pregnant before marriage was a class-A scandal. Boys sneaked peeks at magazines called *Police Gazette* or *True Stories*.

Twin Citians believed strongly in education, mistrusted the rich and felt that minorities should have a place—and stay in it.

They were basically small-town people in a bigger town. They were very patriotic, thought conscientious objectors should be deported and that burning the American flag, much less wearing it on the seat of your pants, was high treason.

Women were content to be in the home, as wives and mothers, and thought that women who worked outside the home were hussies. All in all, they were quiet, relaxed times.

Those times are long over. A disastrous war in Vietnam, a youth revolution, a relaxation in religion and sympathy for things like abortion had their effect. So did the feminist movement, the gay movement and television.

Today it would be difficult, if not impossible, to define Twin Citians. The small-town mentality has given way to a more cosmopolitan one.

Many of the old traits still exist: hardworking, loving the outdoors, believing in education. Many still live in single-family dwellings, but they are not necessarily married.

Church-going has decreased and there are adult book stores and theaters that show hard-core pornography.

Homicides have risen sharply, especially in Minneapolis. In 1947, there were 12 homicides. In 1987, there were 40. St. Paul had only three killings in 1947, and 12 in 1987.

A solitary pedestrian strolls Sixth Street in Minneapolis—passing the City Center.

Facing page: *Downtown Minneapolis as viewed from the Pillsbury Tower.* STEVE SCHNEIDER PHOTOS

Hate crimes have risen markedly in Minnesota, mainly in the Twin Cities area. In 1987, there were 29 acts of anti-Semitism in the state—tying it for 10th in the United States. Five attempted bombings and arsons occurred that year—half of all such acts in the nation.

Said Stephen Cooper, Minnesota Human Rights Commissioner: there's "a lot of hate activity" in the state. While there is not much community support for hate activity, he said, Jews, blacks, Hispanics, Indians, gays and lesbians face "a climate of hate."

Drug busts for cocaine are not uncommon. And children can buy marijuana from people who hang around school yards. Children even are selling it themselves.

Instant communication throughout the world and international travel to and from the Twin Cities have taken away the sense of being isolated from the rest of humanity.

By New York or San Francisco standards, Twin Citians still are on the conservative side. But not nearly as much these days. Visitors still experience friendliness, if they stay out of certain neighborhoods, and still feel the sense of open space in the cities.

Politically, Twin Citians always have been unpredictable. They have voted for Republicans for governor (Luther Youngdahl, Harold Stassen, Al Quie) and Democrats for governor (Floyd Olson, Wendell Anderson and the current governor, Rudy Perpich). The present U.S. senators, Dave Durenberger and Rudy Boschwitz are Republicans, but in the past there have been Democrats such as Walter Mondale and Hubert Humphrey in those posts.

Where legal gambling once was condemned as a tool of the devil, the cities now have Canterbury Downs, a full-scale horse racing track. And the state is seriously considering a lottery. Illegal gambling, mainly on sports, is a multimillion-dollar business in the cities.

Cultural aspects of the area have grown immensely. There are more legitimate theater, art galleries and music, both popular and classical.

Since the early 1960s, professional sports have taken a strong hold: in baseball, the Minnesota Twins; in football, the Minnesota Vikings; in hockey, the North Stars; in soccer, the Strikers. And in 1989 or 1990, there will be a professional basketball team, the Timberwolves.

An article in the Minneapolis *Star Tribune* reported that the average Twin Cities area household includes a married couple in their early to mid-30s, with one child or none and a total yearly income of about $30,000.

The family lives in a 35-year-old house with three bedrooms and a 1987 market value of $78,500. They spend between $300 and $350 a month on food and eat out two or three times a month.

The article was compiled with the help of the Metropolitan Council, Minnesota Builders Association, National Association of Home Builders, U.S. Census Bureau, Minnesota Demographer's Office, among other institutions.

It reports that both adults in the household are high school graduates and have at least attended college. The study continues:

"They are most likely to work in managerial, professional, technical, sales or support jobs…Their mortgage payment is about $500 a month, and they pay $1,200 a year for natural gas and electricity…The house has a single garage, no garage door opener, although the latter probably will be added before long.

"Furnishings don't follow any particular style, and were chosen for comfort, not style or show…There are some consumer goods our average—or median, or archetypical—couple is certain to own. Among them are two cars, a microwave oven, 35mm camera, a push lawn-mower (probably power, but not self-propelled), a stereo and records, a cassette recorder and audio tapes, two telephones, two TV sets (one may be black-and-white), camping equipment, fishing and/or hunting equipment, one or two bicycles…

"The average Twin Cities-area resident takes at least one business or personal trip on an airline each year, and at least one trip out of Minnesota…And our average Twin Citians devote less than two hours a day to television, which is below norm for most metropolitan areas.

The Seasons

A wag once quipped: "You can do everything in the Twin Cities except get lost." There's truth in that. It's an area that a Renaissance person could cherish. But it's an easily understandable area.

In summer, the region provides swimming in its spring-fed lakes. Also sailboating, wind surfing, canoeing and fishing. A significant number of Twin Citians own cabins on the shores of northern Minnesota lakes, where weekends are spent fishing and boating.

Many of the Twin Cities lakes also provide paths for jogging, biking, roller skating and just plain walking. There are launches for romantic moonlight rides and, between Lake Harriet and Lake Calhoun in Minneapolis, is an old-fashioned streetcar ride. Harriet also has summer-night band and orchestra concerts.

Then there are the summer festivals. The major summer event in Minneapolis is the Aquatennial, the largest civic summer festival in the nation. The nine-day July celebration of water has been held for 48 years and includes a day and a night parade, hot-air ballooning, rafting and motorboat racing on the Mississippi River, milk-carton boat races on Lake Calhoun and many other events.

St. Paul has its Riverfest, a 10-day July event on the Mississippi at Harriet Island. It sports a midway, thrill show, music, mimes, clowns, towboat and sternwheeler races and a daily boat parade. Three stages feature music by such as Bruce Willis, Whitney Houston and Survivor and Starship, among many others.

For the more classical types, there is Sommerfest, a series of Minnesota Orchestra concerts at Orchestra Hall and nearby Peavey Plaza. The festival begins July 15 and continues for 25 days. There are dancing under the stars, Viennese food and the music of Mozart, Beethoven, Verdi, Tchaikovsky and others.

Interest in the Minnesota Twins baseball team has rocketed since the team won the World Series in 1987. The original controversy over playing in the Metrodome, instead of in an open park, has diminished.

As autumn nears, team sports begin. No child, it seems, is too young to take part. Little League. Peewee League. Park Board Leagues. Football, baseball, hockey, soccer. Parents take an active part in the organized sports.

In most cases, the emphasis is on teaching teamwork and sportsmanship. Winning is nice, but not everything.

The fall is also time for high school and college sports. The University of Minnesota Golden Gopher football team regularly fills the Metrodome. Football at high schools and smaller colleges in the area also draws big crowds. Amateur baseball has traditionally not drawn heavily, but basketball is very popular. Soccer is growing as a Twin Cities area sport.

Deeper into autumn, a wonderland of color appears as the leaves on the thousands of trees in the Twin Cities area turn from green to shades of orange and red and, finally, brown.

Hunting is a big sport in the fall. Ducks. Geese, including Canadian honkers. Pheasants. Deer. Except under special circumstances, hunting is not allowed within the cities—although, for instance, there are many deer ranging the area. But many Twin Citians travel the state in search of wild game.

In winter, the lakes provide a surface for skating and iceboating and fishing. Fishermen sitting out on a lake looking through a hole in the ice are a common winter sight.

In recent years, many Twin Citians have adopted the "winter beater" principle. They park their regular cars and start using a cheap car (a "beater")—thus saving their good car from the ravages of winter. Said Alex Johnson, sales manager for Terry Feldmann Imports: "People store their good car, put it away like a bear going into hibernation."

The biggest winter show in the area is the St. Paul Winter Carnival, a celebration designed to take the fear out

The St. Paul Winter Carnival is a celebration designed to take the fear out of cold weather.

of cold weather. King Boreas, usually a prominent St. Paulite, reigns over the carnival as the monarch of winter until he is attacked by Vulcan, portrayed by another prominent St. Paulite, the master of fire and heat.

The famous Ice Palace of the St. Paul Winter Carnival has been built for many carnivals in January near the shore of Lake Phelan. Thousands yearly visit the carnival and the huge ice sculptures—both of which have been nationally acclaimed.

As the snow deepens, people take to their sleds and toboggans and, mainly, to their skis. There are skiing facilities in the area, but it is common for the city people to travel outstate or as far as Colorado and the mountains of California to satisfy their lust for skiing. Some of the more affluent go to the Swiss Alps. And, long a tradition, have been the horse-drawn sleigh rides, with kids bouncing on the hay atop the sleighs and lovers going for the midnight rides.

The Twin Cities winters are long. That doesn't bother the sports types. But it can be hard for some, especially the elderly. Thus, spring is always most welcome.

The cycle of growth begins again, with flowers emerging from the earth and the temperatures become tolerable without a heavy overcoat.

It's back to walking, jogging, roller skating, boating and the other activities mostly denied in winter.

Left: *The horse-and-buggy rides of the St. Paul Winter Carnival are trips into the past.* MICHAEL MAGNUSON

Facing page: *St. Paul's Ordway Music Theatre, a symbol of the people getting involved.* STEVE SCHNEIDER

A view of the thrust stage of the Guthrie Theater, where plays range from Moliere to Guys and Dolls. *This production is Shakespeare's* Richard III.

Facing page: *Many come to St. Paul just to see the architecture of the Ordway Music Theatre.*
STEVE SCHNEIDER PHOTOS

The Arts

Twin Citians love their theater and music. They support some 20 legitimate theaters, ranging from small houses to the prestigious Guthrie Theater. Others include Actors Theater, in St. Paul, and Theatre in the Round and Children's Theatre Company, in Minneapolis.

More specialized are theaters with names such as Theatre de la Jeune Lune, Mixed Blood, Brass Tacks, Penumbra and At the Foot of the Mountain.

For music, there are the two main houses: Orchestra Hall and the Ordway Music Theatre. Major organizations include the Minnesota Orchestra and the Saint Paul Chamber Orchestra. But there are many small places for music: bars, restaurants, nightclubs and the like.

Art also plays an important role in the cities' culture. Major art houses are the Minneapolis Institute of Art, Walker Art Center and the Minnesota Museum of Art.

The Guthrie

With spotlights and international attention, the Guthrie Theater opened May 7, 1963. It was the dream of the British director, Sir Tyrone Guthrie, who wanted something unique to bear his name.

Guthrie came to Minneapolis in 1962 to create one of America's first permanent regional theater companies. He was known for his imagination and willingness to experiment. He said he wanted in Minneapolis "a long-term policy, concerned with establishing a classical repertory company, with strong local attachments, aiming gradually to achieve its own distinctive style. The purpose of all this is to be of some service to the American theater at large, but especially do we aim to be of use to the community which has called us into being and supports us."

The theater, seating 1,437, has a thrust stage, with the people sitting in a horseshoe-shaped auditorium around it. No one is far from the stage.

It was truly a community project. All the $1.2 million to build the theater came from firms and the people.

It is located on the northern end of Kenwood across from Parade Stadium, where for years high school football games have been played.

Sir Tyrone himself directed the first production, *Hamlet* in modern dress. This and other productions have drawn national attention in magazines and newspapers.

In keeping with its heartland-of-America purpose, the Guthrie has taken the theater's productions to smaller communities. John Steinbeck's *Of Mice and Men,* for instance, toured 15 towns in Minnesota, Iowa, Nebraska, Wisconsin and the Dakotas.

At first, the theater company stuck doggedly to Sir Tyrone's idea of classical productions of playwrights such as Chekhov, Shakespeare and O'Neill. Guthrie died in 1971 and, in later years, the Guthrie on occasion has done popular plays such as *Guys and Dolls* and Cole Porter's *Anything Goes.*

Minnesota Orchestra

When the Germans and Scandinavians came to Minnesota, they brought their love of music with them. In the 1850s, they organized church choirs, parlor concerts, community sings and other musical events.

The first major group was formed in 1882 and called itself the Great Western Band of Minneapolis. That was the historical setting from which evolved the Minneapolis

Symphony Orchestra in 1903—the predecessor of the Minnesota Orchestra.

The Minneapolis Symphony was the fruit of a marriage of a 16-member orchestra and the Filharmonix, a glee club that also featured banjo and mandolin.

Today, the Minnesota Orchestra plays regularly to packed houses and easily is one of the nation's top-ranked symphony orchestras.

By the 1981-82 season, 96 percent of all available seats were sold on subscription—18,000 subscribers in all. The orchestra takes on a heavy schedule: 219 concerts, including a 24-week subscription season, Weekender Pops and Night at the Pops series, the summer festival, free concerts in the parks, Family and Young People's series, and regional and national tours. One outdoor performance of John Philip Sousa marches drew 250,000 people.

The orchestra has premiered works by Bela Bartok, Charles Ives, Dominick Argento and Aaron Copland. A highlight each year is the orchestra's performance of Handel's *Messiah*. The orchestra has had prestigious music directors, including Dimitri Mitropoulos, Eugene Ormandy, Antal Dorati and Sir Neville Marriner and, presently, Edo de Waart.

After many years in Northrop Auditorium on the University of Minnesota campus, the orchestra moved to a new home: the $9.5 million Orchestra Hall in Minneapolis.

Winner of many awards, the orchestra has come a long way from the Great Western Band of Minneapolis.

Saint Paul Chamber Orchestra

In 1959, 24 free-lance musicians got together to form the St. Paul Philharmonic. Leopold Sipe, a local music teacher, was selected as the first conductor. No one dreamed their group would evolve into one of the best of its kind in the world.

The original idea was to perform for young musicians, and thus inspire and teach them. The group also wanted to perform new creations.

It was only a part-time project, but it caught on and, by 1966, it was boasting a 10-concert season. That same year, the Philharmonic made its East Coast debut in the Grand Ballroom of New York's Biltmore Hotel.

Interest in the organization grew and so did the group: it now had 22 members. Two years later it became the first full-time chamber orchestra in the United States. The name was changed to Saint Paul Chamber Orchestra.

In its first full-time season, the orchestra made an East Coast tour, topped off with a performance in New York's Carnegie Hall. Reports an orchestra spokesman: "The New York critics praised the 'sparkling performances' and noted St. Paul's emergence from the cultural shadow of its sister city, Minneapolis."

Under Conductor Dennis Russell Davies, who took over in 1971 at age 28, the orchestra won the 1979 Grammy Award for best classical recording of the year: Aaron Copland's *Appalachian Spring*.

Its best-known director was Pinchas Zukerman, who expanded the season to 85 concerts. He resigned in June of 1987, and the orchestra, which performs now in the Ordway Music Theatre, is searching for a new leader.

Minneapolis Institute of Art

During the 1986-1987 season, the Minneapolis Institute of Art had an attendance of more than a quarter million people. It is the only encyclopedic museum of art in the Upper Midwest.

The institute was founded in 1883 on a shoestring. There was no building: a committee was appointed to find "suitable rooms" for displaying pictures. Another committee was to "call at various stores and secure the services of young men to drape the walls."

On opening day, people had to pay a quarter to get in for what was called the "Art Loan Exhibition." That's because all the art was borrowed, mainly from people in the Twin Cities. The main art work was a painting by Murillo. And the "largest exhibition up to that time" also included the first public showing of the collection of Empire Builder James J. Hill.

Today, the institute is considered one of the leading art centers in the nation. More than 80,000 art objects are in the collection, which represents the history of art from 25,000 B.C.

Its major works include Rembrandt's *Lucretia*, Nicolas Poussin's *The Death of Germanicus,* Rene Magritte's *Les Promenades d'Euclide,* the Pillsbury collection of ancient Chinese bronzes and Paul Revere's silver Templeman Tea Service.

In his 1986-87 annual report, Alan Shestak, institute director, reported the impact of the museum in human terms:

"How does one explain the joy of the museum staff at seeing a young child respond with enthusiasm and delight to a docent tour? And how can one express the sense of gratification at seeing a group of people with impaired hearing getting a signed tour of the museum? How does one communicate the sense of vitality and activity signified by 1,777 bookings of rooms and meeting places within 12 months?…What is clear is that the museum is much used and much enjoyed by the community."

Walker Art Center

In the same building complex as the Guthrie Theater is the Walker Art Center, a home for music and dance concerts, experimental theater, innovative and avant-garde movies, as well as art.

It was founded by Thomas Barlow Walker, an Ohio-born lumber king who, in 1923, had become one of the nation's 10 wealthiest men. He began his art collection in the mid-1870s, with works by George Inness, Thomas Cole and Rembrandt Peale.

He built a gallery between his house and a carriage house in 1879, and established the Walker Art Gallery in 1927. A few months later, he died at age 87.

The present building was opened in 1971 and expanded in 1983. Said the *New York Times:*

"Fifteen years after its completion, [the Walker)]remains not only the best museum designed by Edward Larrabee Barnes, but one of the finest museums for the display of modern art in the nation."

In its permanent collection, the Walker has major examples of European modernism, cubism, abstract expressionism, pop, social realism and minimalism.

It has had exhibitions of artists including Claes Oldenburg, Willem de Kooning, Alexander Calder, Henri Matisse and Picasso.

Minnesota Museum of Art

The origin of the Minnesota Museum of Art goes back to 1890 when artists and community leaders formed something called the Northwest Academy of Arts. Important in those days was a ceramics club.

In 1894, the ceramics club was reorganized into the Saint Paul School of Fine Arts, with evening classes for young men and day classes for women. There were three teachers and about 100 students who met in the Metropolitan Hotel.

One of the most influential backers of art at the time was Mrs. I.R.N. Barber, who became director of the school in 1895. But two years later, she committed suicide and the school was closed.

It was resurrected in 1898. There followed a series of different art schools until the Saint Paul Art Center emerged. It became the Minnesota Museum of Art in 1969, and later it moved into the historic Landmark Center.

Now more than 60 years old, the museum features traveling exhibitions and contemporary artists from the Upper Midwest. Its paintings range from portraits to photographs. Said M.J. Czarniecki III, museum director:

"Renewal in the Museum most often results from self-examination; on retreat in November 1986, the trustees and staff revisited MMA's mission statement. From that beginning and subsequent study, a revised and embellished statement of mission was adopted in March. It expands the Museum's focus to collect, preserve and exhibit American art from all periods; it targets the Museum's primary audience as Minnesotans; it reaffirms the Museum's educational purpose."

A Minneapolis commercial building with wall mural.

Facing page: *Every game of the Minnesota Vikings (shown playing the Washington Redskins) sells out the Metrodome.* STEVE SCHNEIDER PHOTOS

43

Above: *A popular contest of the Minneapolis Aquatennial, a summer festival, is creating sand castles.* MICHAEL MAGNUSON

Right: *A scene on the Mississippi River, below the University of Minnesota.* STEVE SCHNEIDER

Twin Cities' Minorities

The major problem concerning minorities in the Twin Cities area is the misplaced sense of whites that everything is O.K. We have the capability to eliminate the problem, but we never do that because we think we already have. It's like the guy who didn't change the oil in his car because he thought he already had. Sooner or later, there will be a cost.

—Stephen W. Cooper, Minnesota Human Rights Commissioner

Minnesota's minority population is only about 3.8 percent of total state population and most members of minorities live in the Twin Cities metro area. Latest figures available (1985) show an estimated 154,500 nonwhites in the state, with 4,038,500 whites.

The largest minority is black (72,700) and a smaller group is the Asians (39,700), but the numbers of Asians have grown faster in recent years than those of any other race or ethnic group.

There has been integration in city public schools, but very little in the suburbs. And, for the most part, members of minorities live in segregated neighborhoods. The number of minority teachers in the state is less than 2 percent, and has been at that mark since 1980. There are no black members of the Minnesota Legislature.

There is little outward hatred, but there is a complacence among whites, according to Stephen W. Cooper, state Human Rights commissioner:

"We don't have the animosity, hate and collision as in eastern cities such as Detroit and Philadelphia and Atlanta where as much as half the population is minority. They have had to learn to share power in those cities, but we haven't.

"We have the paternalistic approach of giving power rather than sharing it. Our minority population is not large enough to have political clout. They have moral clout, but that's not as powerful as votes. The minorities get the worst of things: worst schools, worst housing, worst jobs, worst hospital care, worst police protection.

"Our older white people think lack of prejudice means 'I'll let you be like me.' Lack of prejudice doesn't mean 'I'll allow you to be another white guy.' The kids growing up in integrated schools, however, tend to have a different attitude. They say, 'You can be like me if you want to, but you can be like you, too.'

Hmong people and other Southeast Asians have settled largely in St. Paul. They are the most victimized, contends Cooper. They are small in stature, tend to live in tough neighborhoods, often can't speak the language and don't know the customs.

Members of minorities in the Twin Cities area, however, have taken significant roles in community life. They have been elected to city councils, have joined the police forces and, in the inner cities, are active in public school life.

Said Cooper: "An active minority person is as likely to be totally involved in non-minority issues as they are in minority issues. They play very important roles in society in general."

There have been efforts to teach about minority groups in schools. St. Paul and Minneapolis public schools, for instance, must teach the various cultures under state mandate. Such action was prompted by discoveries such as that many elementary schoolchildren didn't know that American Indians were in this country before whites arrived.

Since the mid-1970s, more than 100,000 Southeast Asian refugee children have attended Minnesota public schools, mostly in the Twin Cities area. Hundreds have enrolled in special language classes.

In 1986, Shoua Cha, son of a Laotian priest, became the first Southeast Asian to be sworn in as a city policeman. He first was on the Minneapolis force and then, under a lateral hiring provision of Civil Service, transferred to St. Paul.

But, despite some progress, there is a long way to go. Concludes Commissioner Cooper:

"The most frustrating thing is the tremendous degree to which problems have remained unsolved. We said we will take the problems of minorities seriously as long as it doesn't require us to sacrifice anything."

Talking Minnesotan

Do Minnesotans have a language of their own? You bet.

If you grow up in the Twin Cities, you don't notice the Minnesota language. But Howard Mohr did.

Mohr, a writer for Garrison Keillor's radio show, "A Prairie Home Companion," discusses the language in his book, *How to Talk Minnesotan*. He writes:

"Minnesotan is not a musical language. Some people with an ax to grind have said it is the musical equivalent of a one-string guitar. What I say is, what's wrong with a monotone—at least you don't startle anybody…"

"You bet," for instance, has more than one meaning, contends Mohr. It can be in response to a thank you. Or it can be in response to a question.

"Warm enough for you?"

"You bet."

For Mohr, a "heckuva deal" is the biggest deal of all. "On that Oldsmobile of mine, you know, I'm gettin' about thirty miles to the gallon in town. Not too bad a deal, huh?"

"That's a heckuva deal if you ask me."

Mohr also gets into the phenomenon of lutefisk, a fish that has no in-between supporters. You love it or you hate it. There are a thousand jokes about the dish. One is cited by Mohr:

"This Minnesotan, see, invites some friends over for a lutefisk feed, and just as they get inside the door, there's this gigantic explosion that lifts off the roof of the kitchen and sets fire to the curtains. "Pull up a chair," the guy says. "The lutefisk is done."

You bet. Heckuva deal.

Sommerfest, Aquatennial and Riverfest are highlights of the summertime.

Upper left: Many Indians in the Twin Cities maintain traditional ways. Here is a scene of the Heart o' Earth Powwow.
Above: Snow is part of the life of Twin Citians, who know how to deal with it.
Far left: Thousands of Twin Citians ice skate on area lakes and park ponds.
Left: The Lake Harriet bandshell—a place where Minneapolis area people gather for outdoor music.

Facing page: On the banks of the Mississippi is Riverplace—a building of specialty shops and restaurants.
STEVE SCHNEIDER PHOTOS

CHAPTER 3

MINNEAPOLIS HISTORY

Above: *Settlers brought New England industriousness and culture to the plains. This is the World Theater.*
Right: *St. Anthony Falls was the beginning of the city of Minneapolis. It generated the first major industry: lumbering.* STEVE SCHNEIDER PHOTOS

The Indians knew about it, but it wasn't until 1680 that St. Anthony Falls was discovered for the white world by Father Hennepin, the Franciscan priest and explorer. He had no idea then that the falls would create the city of Minneapolis.

The 16-foot falls are deep in Indian legend. In her book, *The Waterfall That Built a City,* Lucile. M. Kane tells the tale of Ampato Sapa, the wife of a Sioux hunter and mother of a small son. Her husband, to show off his prosperity, decided to take a second wife.

Ampato was crushed, but kept silent. When spring came, she dressed in her bridal robe and, with her child, got into a canoe above the falls. Singing her death song, Ampato paddled the canoe past her husband watching from shore. The canoe sailed over the falls and into the churning waters below. Her lament is said to be heard in the winds above the falls.

The falls remained relatively unknown until Fort Snelling was established in the 1820s. Then people began to come up the Mississippi by the 1850s and the falls became a famed tourist attraction.

While most saw the falls as a thing of beauty, some—including the state's first governor, Henry Sibley—envisioned it as a source of power to exploit for profit.

Lumbering became the first big industry generated by the falls. In the mid-1850s, sawmills increased from one to four. Then, in 1851, the first flour mill was established, a small grist mill that some laughed at. The soil in the region was perfect for growing wheat and other grains.

The population grew: from about 300 in 1848 to 3,000 seven years later. Minneapolis was born in 1854. The real booms in both flour milling and population growth would follow the Civil War.

The population figures at times were suspect. For instance, on the rolls, was: "Hans Von Sphikenshpokenblungg, Main Street near Sidewalk." Somehow, they never could find him.

Many of the inhabitants came from the East Coast, including New England. They gave the region its first semblance of culture and gentility—meager as it was in the beginning. Those seeds of social class, however, were to develop into what some call the Paris of the Plains.

From the New Englanders came piety and Puritanism. A law banning work, shooting, hunting and sports on Sunday was passed by the first state legislature (1858). Later, it was forbidden to dance or go to shows on Sunday.

Among the first New Englanders were lumberman Caleb Dorr, Dr. Alfred Ames, the city's first physician, Ard Godfrey, the first millwright in Minneapolis, and pioneer mill owners William D. and Cadwallader Washburn and the Pillsbury family.

Col. John H. Stevens had built the first house in what would become Minneapolis during the winter of 1849-1850. It became the town's community center and included the post office and general store.

Scandinavians eventually came by the thousands. So did the Germans and Irish. They were hard-working, conservative people who worked in the mills. They loved their new country and they believed in education.

Minneapolis began with the small settlement of St. Anthony just east of the Mississippi, in 1849. The land west of the river, land containing Fort Snelling and owned by the federal government, was Indian land not opened to settlement until after the Treaty of Traverse des Sioux in 1851.

The Mississippi, and its problems, made the residents of Minneapolis a closer society. They needed each other. In 1869, an attempt to build a tunnel under Nicollet and Hennepin islands led to disastrous erosion that threatened the falls itself. Side by side, the citizens—mill owners and workers alike—rushed to fill in the collapsed tunnel. Nicollet Island, near the falls, was almost wiped out. The disaster required building a concrete dam over the falls, two low dams and a bypass channel, between 1870 and 1884.

A battle for economic power, combined with population growth, highlighted the second half of the 19th century. Money was solicited from the East, mainly New York City, by men—including John S. Pillsbury and the Washburns—who saw the potential of a city rich with milling. They were not men out for a fast buck. They figured that their investment in Minneapolis would be long-term and that they would become a vital part of the development of the city. By 1870, the population was more than 13,000.

William Washburn's background was typical of early Minneapolis adventurers. It was described in *History of the City of Minneapolis* (1893), edited by Isaac Atwater:

"The ancestors of the Washburn family were of the brave old Pilgrim stock and dwelt in the quiet little English village of Evesham, near the Avon, Shakespeare's river. When the days grew evil in England, John Washburn, sec-

Minneapolis's early immigrants were hard-working and conservative, and they loved their new country.

Above: *The city of Minneapolis today at dawn.* STEVE SCHNEIDER
Right: *Its first non-Indian visitor, Father Louis Hennepin.* COURTESY MINNESOTA HISTORICAL SOCIETY

Facing page: *The empire-builder, James J. Hill.* COURTESY MINNESOTA HISTORICAL SOCIETY

retary of the Plymouth colony in England, sailed across the sea to Massachusetts…"

His descendant, William Drew Washburn, came to Minneapolis in 1857:

"At the age of twenty-six, endowed with a vigorous constitution, a liberal education and a legal diploma, he sought a place to settle and enter upon his life work.

"The examples of brothers who had attained eminence, the one in the state of his birth, and others at the West, were before him and no doubt stimulated him to do his utmost to honor the name already famous throughout the country. He decided in favor of the West and determined to settle at the Falls of St. Anthony…

"It required no prophetic gift to foresee that here would grow up a prosperous community, and perchance become the 'seat of Empire'…

Washburn was elected to the U.S. House of Representatives in 1878, and later to the Senate, and he devoted most of his attention to Minneapolis. Through his efforts, Minneapolis received a federal courts building and post office and a system of reservoirs for the Mississippi River.

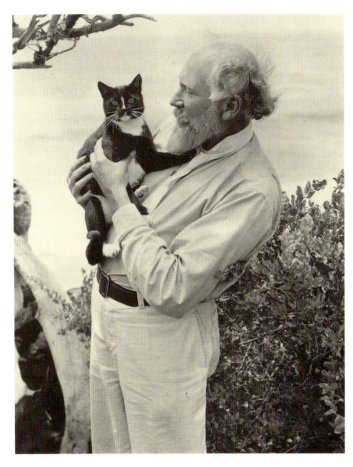

The city was beginning its adolescence. Slowly, the dirt roads of "downtown" Minneapolis were converted to streets and avenues. Hennepin Avenue, named after the Franciscan explorer-priest, Fr. Louis Hennepin, looked like a typical western frontier street during the 1860s. But it sported an opera house and a, for those days, majestic hotel. There was, of course, a proper sprinkling of saloons.

Construction of the major flour mills that were to make Minneapolis famous began in the last quarter of the 19th century. In 1874, the Washburn A Mill was opened; seven years later the Pillsburys constructed Mill A for the substantial sum of $500,000.

Minneapolitans proved to be tough-minded and could bounce back from disaster like punching-bag dolls.

In 1870, a row of sawmills was destroyed by fire when workman tried to fill a kerosene lamp with its wick afire. It exploded and soon the mills were gone.

And, in 1878, the original Washburn A Mill had its own disaster. Four years after it started putting out a third of the area's flour, it exploded. Eighteen men were killed.

But the people survived the disasters. There seemed to be a desire to make something out of the rugged city they cherished. Hardly anyone would pack up and desert the place.

The competition and animosity involving Minneapolis and St. Paul have diminished through the years. But it was very strong during the early days. There was a long census war during which both cities claimed to have the most people. That climaxed in 1890: census takers were kidnapped and the count was padded.

When James J. Hill, the famed railroad builder, bought half the St. Anthony power supply in 1880, the *St. Paul Daily Globe* had a headline reading: "Here She Booms. St. Paul Buys Out Minneapolis for $425,000."

Hill, the son of a Canadian farmer, left home at about 15 to make his fortune. He was a a short, thick man with a large head, long black hair and a blind eye. Stern, he was like a grim old lion in later years.

In 1856, nearly 18 years old, Hill had arrived in St. Paul, then a town of about 6,000, and became involved in various businesses before acquiring the bankrupt St. Paul and Pacific railroad with three partners.

The first railroad in Minnesota was only 10 miles long—from St. Paul to Minneapolis on the east side of the Mississippi. It was constructed in 1862 and didn't reach across the river until 1867, when a bridge was completed.

After long labor, Hill created the Great Northern railroad, which eventually stretched from the Twin Cities to the West Coast, in 1893. He availed himself of 44 million acres in federal land grants and spent only about $28,000 per mile of track. That was never equaled by any other national railroad.

Hill was a man with a vision. And he loved the Twin Cities area. He owned a farm, which is now a wealthy suburb, North Oaks, where he bred fine polled Black Angus beef cattle and shorthorn dairy cattle. His plan was to assist agricultural diversification in Minnesota and the Dakotas, which in turn would benefit his railroad.

The early Minneapolitans desired to make something out of the rugged city they cherished.

51

The railroads were important to the flour milling. Shipping during the steamboat navigation season was no longer essential. And, of course, immigrants followed the railroads west.

One reason for the swelling population of Minneapolis had been free advertising beginning in the 1850s. Traveling writers had described the city's Upper Mississippi scenery as if it were Paris in the spring or the Blue Danube in the fall. The Falls of St. Anthony, although much smaller, were described as second only to Niagara. Stories and, eventually, advertising, appeared in American magazines, newspapers and books and even in European publications, particularly in England and Germany. Immigration agents recruited new residents on the East Coast and in Europe.

At one point, before trains became dominant, one needed to travel from New York City by train to Chicago, at a cost of $10, then take a stage to the river for $8, then a boat to St. Paul ($6 for first-class). Total: an exorbitant $24.

The Civil War didn't help Minneapolis. The city sent about 1,400 volunteers to fight for the North—a much larger percentage of population than most cities.

At Gettysburg, eight companies of the First Minnesota Regiment, mostly from Minneapolis and St. Paul, were ordered to charge two Confederate brigades. They were outnumbered 20 to one. They were successful, but, out of 262 men, 215 were killed or wounded. Gen. Winfield Scott Hancock later said:

"There is no more gallant deed recorded in history. I ordered these men in there because I needed five minutes time. Reinforcements were coming on the run, but I knew that before they could reach the threatened point, the Confederates, unless checked, would seize the position. I would have ordered that regiment in if I had known that every man would be killed. It had to be done. And I was glad to have such a gallant body of men at hand, willing to make the terrible sacrifice that the occasion demanded."

Somehow the war was survived, along with the Panic of 1857 and the Sioux War of 1862. The people who had chosen to settle in Minneapolis seemed to have similar qualities: resourcefulness, patience, loyalty and guts.

One object of the industrious Minneapolitans was to outproduce St. Louis, Missouri, then known as "the queen flour city of America." They succeeded in 1880, when Minneapolis produced 2,051,840 barrels of flour. That was

more than $20 million worth. Minneapolis was "queen flour city" for the next 50 years.

To serve the growing population of Minneapolis, there was an influx of merchants, teachers, lawyers, doctors and bankers, among other professionals. By 1890, the city claimed more than 164,000 residents.

Now, it was time to construct big buildings, replacing the more-or-less temporary ones that the settlers had built. The first *skyscraper* was the Guaranty Loan Building—all of 12 stories high—in the early 1880s. But for Minneapolis that was magnificent. After all, the Guaranty Loan had electric lights and turkish baths and a string orchestra that played on the roof deck.

In the book *Pioneer Harvest,* Marion E. Cross describes that era of building :

"Minneapolis had had a number of building booms but none have left such a stamp on the city and none have remained so easily recognizable…By the end of the 1880s such a change had come over the business section that anyone who had been absent from the city for ten years would have been bewildered by the transformation…The downtown area looked wonderfully spruced up with is new cement sidewalks and its curbs and gutters and paved streets…Only a person who had known the city in its pre-boom days could fully appreciate the psychological change that had gone hand in hand with the coming of age…"

"Coming of age" so quickly was to hurt the city. The Panic of 1893 threw Minneapolis into a depression that was devastating. Two banks—Citizens Bank and Northwestern Guaranty Loan Co.—collapsed within a week. A run at Farmers and Mechanics Savings Bank brought out the police. People literally climbed over others, trying to be first in line. The depositors were paid off in gold coin,

The Armistice Day blizzard in 1940 meant one-lane traffic for a while—and then only on major streets.

Facing page: *John Sargent Pillsbury, savior of the University of Minnesota.* PHOTOS COURTESY MINNESOTA HISTORICAL SOCIETY

and those with several thousand dollars found they couldn't lift that much gold.

But, again, the hardy Minneapolitans survived. Prosperity returned at the beginning of the 20th century.

Horses were important to the development of Minneapolis. They pulled fire wagons and the first streetcars, and surreys "with isinglass windows you can roll right down." Minneapolitans treated the thought of horseless carriages with the same enthusiasm as root canal dentistry.

The first automobile in Minneapolis was driven, with great pride, by Swan Turnblad, a Swedish newspaper publisher, in 1895. But it was years before the "thing" began to be accepted.

After all, it was not Minneapolis. It was a foreign product. But the Minneapolitans survived the car, and reluctantly they gave in.

They were more in tune with the Minneapolis of 1901, as described in *Pioneer Harvest* The city then claimed a population of 300,000:

"The scent of new-baked bread was a familiar one in those days…Milk did not come in bottles. The men brought it in a milk can and deep foam rose as it was poured into whatever pitcher or bowl was handy. In winter the milk came out as frozen slush, and wonderful pretend-ice cream it was for the children. There were no cans or sacks of coffee on grocery store shelves. The grocer ground coffee beans in a big machine for each customer and he always gave some penny candy to any child who was brought to the store

"In winter the streets rang with sleigh bells which, to children, meant a chance to hook a ride on a delivery sleigh. After a snowstorm, sidewalks were cleared by horse-drawn snowplows. Those were the days when none but children skied, and skiing meant sliding downhill and trudging back uphill, skis in hand.

"Summertime meant sprinkling cans and ice wagons, the whistle of the popcorn man on his slow round, fire horses dashing by on their daily runs for exercise. There were organ-grinders with monkeys, and scissors-grinders and junk men and fruit peddlers. And there were extras that newsboys were always shouting."

Characteristic of the growth of Minneapolis at the turn of the century was the West Hotel on Hennepin Avenue. Built in 1884, it helped shape the business and social life of the city. Presidents slept there: Taft, Wilson, Teddy

Roosevelt. So did the Lord Mayor of Dublin and billionaire J. Paul Getty.

It was frequented by the highest society of the region. The wealthy social elite gathered in its fancy ballrooms. And the West had its scandal: a wealthy playboy was stabbed to death in the billiard room. The site of the hotel is a parking lot now.

Although Minneapolitans were becoming sophisticated, they didn't abandon their small-town values. The people were determined that their city would have space and beauty and a healthful environment. They created parks and drained swamps to make lakes amidst them. The string of parks was reserved for fun and games and for children and the elderly.

The fervent attitude toward education of the early settlers never was lost. And, in February of 1851, the University of Minnesota was born. Many thought it would not last until spring. As James Gray wrote in *University of Minnesota—1851-1951:* "To read the records of the first years of the University of Minnesota—created in a great flash of altruistic enthusiasm and very nearly eclipsed within a decade—is to have the impression of having been transported into a world utterly unlike one's own, of being flung precipitately onto a white-hot star whirling through an unfamiliar element at the very moment of creation."

But create it they did, and it was destined to become one of the largest universities in the nation. The first building was a "preparatory department"—offering pre-college classical education—in St. Anthony Falls.

A second site, a mile down the Mississippi, was selected and a much larger building went into construction. Money problems followed and the building was abandoned. S.C. Gale took a Yale classmate to see it and reported that windows were broken and the only tenants were a sow and her litter of pigs.

Regarded as the Father of the University was John Sargent Pillsbury, whose statue stands facing the old library building, now Burton Hall. Although he had no college education, he knew the benefits of one. And he knew that the future of Minneapolis would be shaped by educated people. Born in New Hampshire, Pillsbury had begun working for a living at age 15—first as an apprentice printer and then as a clerk in his brother's store.

In 1862, the university was in a disastrous financial condition. Most leaders of the city thought it would go under. Not Pillsbury. He traveled across the state settling money claims against the university. And he got other business leaders to help him come to the rescue. By 1867, the last claim had been paid.

There is no doubt that the university would have crumbled without Pillsbury. He devoted at least a third of his time to the institution—for no pay—and all of his imagination and creativity. He also donated a $150,000 building.

In 1951, the University of Minnesota was the fourth largest community in the state. What had begun with 20 students now has more than 44,000 at the campuses in Minneapolis and St. Paul and more than 11,000 at its four outstate branches.

One of the best medical schools and hospital was developed at the university. It produced, among others, Dr. Owen Wangensteen, who developed a surgery to remove intestinal obstructions, and Dr. Ancel Keys, who was instrumental in creating the military K-ration. Dr. Alfred Nier, a scientist at the university, was the first to isolate the uranium isotope.

Minneapolis was dominated by the wealthy business community until 1934. On May 21 and 22 of that year, the famous truckers' strike erupted. The truckers of Teamsters Local 574 complained of low pay and long hours and wanted to strengthen their union by showing power and winning the strike.

The 800 employers of the Citizens' Alliance of Minneapolis (an established anti-union group) would have none of that. They established their headquarters in the posh West Hotel, an act that aggravated the situation more. And Minneapolis police made a huge mistake: they deputized the businessmen and sent them out, in plain clothes, to control the strikers. One, Alfred Lindley, a sportsman and mountain climber, didn't help by showing up in jodhpurs and a polo hat. Another business leader arrived wearing a football helmet. Hennepin County Sheriff John Wall called it a horrible mistake. "You see," he said, "the strikers regarded them the same as strikebreakers. But the Chief of Police was hollering for more men so we tried it."

A bloody battle in the streets ensued. There was a clash on May 21, but no one was seriously hurt. Twenty to thirty thousand people, however, showed up the next morning in the market place. A battle was triggered by a minor incident: a small merchant was moving some crates

By the turn of the century, Minneapolitans were becoming sophisticated, but they did not abandon small-town values.

Facing page: *The Guaranty Loan Building's 12 stories provided Minneapolis with its first skyscraper in the 1880s.* COURTESY MINNESOTA HISTORICAL SOCIETY

Teamster Local 574 fought the anti-union Citizens' Alliance of Minneapolis in the streets in May of 1934.

Facing page: *Mayor of Minneapolis Hubert H. Humphrey.* PHOTOS COURTESY MINNESOTA HISTORICAL SOCIETY

of tomatoes, and a striker threw one through a window. The shattering of glass seemed to be a signal for both sides.

Saps, blackjacks, lead pipes and night sticks were used in hand-to-hand combat. The fighting spread to all corners of the city, with the police and their special "deputies" mainly retreating.

There had been tension for months in Minneapolis. The people barely were surviving the Depression and were in no mood for oppression anymore. The union's Farrell Dobbs explained in an interview with Charles Rumford Walker for the book *American City:*

"Instantly it became a free for all. Arthur Lyman [lawyer and vice president of American Ball Co.] was killed while running to cover in a grocery store—between the curb and the door. But it made no difference who (a person) was, provided he had a deputy's badge or a club. Just to show you how dangerous it was to be a deputy, several of our fellows picked up the clubs from fallen deputies, and were immediately knocked cold by pickets. Our boys didn't look in a man's face—all they saw was the club."

Although minor skirmishes continued, the main battle was over in only about an hour. Hundreds lay wounded and another deputy besides Lyman was killed. The truckers had won, but no one was celebrating. The employers agreed to a minimum wage, reinstatement with no discrimination, arbitration for future wage changes, seniority in hiring and layoff. But most important of all was recognition of the truckers' union. It was the beginning of a new Minneapolis with organized labor vital and strong.

But the unions still didn't have an easy time growing. A second street battle, for instance, occurred on Bloody Friday, July 20 of 1934. This time the police were armed. They opened fire on the truckers and, in 10 minutes, two were killed and 67 wounded, including 13 bystanders.

After the 1934 "civil war," Minneapolitans settled down to a peaceful life. They listened to the radio and went to movies. Particularly popular were the Fred Astaire-Ginger Rogers musicals in which the stars wore formal clothes, drank champagne and ate caviar. Few in Minneapolis could afford such a lavish life, but it was fun watching.

People rode streetcars to work, or walked. Those who had cars (you could get a reliable used one for $35) found them too expensive to drive to and from work and to pay for parking.

Crime was rare, particularly violent attacks. So, people felt safe walking about the city at night. There were only a handful of homicides each year. There were some sensational killings. Walter Liggett, editor of a small Minneapolis scandal sheet in which he wrote about underworld activities, was slain by a machinegunner in 1935. Isadore Blumenfeld, better known as Kid Cann, was tried for the murder, but was acquitted.

There were a limited number of liquor licenses available and so they were most valuable. Only one to a customer was allowed. Cann and Tommy Banks were alleged to have gotten several bar licenses, seeking to control the bar industry in Minneapolis.

But, aside from murders such as the Liggett case, the typical killing involved one marriage partner hitting the other over the head with a hammer. No Agatha Christie stuff in Minneapolis. There were patrolmen walking beats in those days, policemen who got to know people. Minneapolis was a middle-class city on the plains—safe from the hustle of the East and West coasts.

Despite World War II, the 1940s in Minneapolis were pleasant and innocent. As in World War I, the city had sent more than its share of young men to war, but otherwise places like Europe and the South Pacific seemed far away indeed.

A young college teacher then took charge of Minneapolis. Hubert H. Humphrey decided to run for mayor in 1945 against the incumbent, Marvin Kline. Prostitution and gambling had moved into the edges of downtown Minneapolis and Kline looked the other way. Humphrey won the election and cleaned up the town in a few months.

It wasn't until much later that he told people how he did it. He called in the police chief and told him to select a squad of big, strong men. They were to run the prostitutes and gamblers out of town. "And I don't want anyone crowding up the jail," said Humphrey. The cops rounded up the suspects and escorted them, with whatever force necessary, to trains and buses. There was some talk by those evicted about violation of civil rights. Humphrey, of course, later went on to be a civil rights leader in the U.S. Senate.

Humphrey's election as mayor began a political dynasty. From his organization came the likes of Walter Mondale, Orville Freeman, Eugene McCarthy and Wendell Anderson.

All of them held national offices. Humphrey and Mondale became senators, then vice presidents. Humphrey, McCarthy and Mondale ran for president (Humphrey and Mondale as Democratic candidates). Freeman was Secretary of Agriculture for John F. Kennedy and Anderson was governor of Minnesota.

As mayor of Minneapolis, Humphrey worked hard to eliminate anti-Semitism and to make the city an equal-opportunity community. He was instrumental in getting the first equal employment commission in the United States located in Minneapolis. The feisty man was re-elected mayor in 1947, but resigned in 1948 to successfully run for the United States Senate.

The move to the suburbs began about 1950—the year Minneapolis had its largest population: 521,718. By the thousands, people, mainly young families formed during the war who could find no housing in the city, moved into the suburbs. Bloomington, a sprawling southern community, grew the most. By 1987, its estimate population estimate reached 84,480. It became Minnesota's third-largest city, edging out Duluth.

57

Minneapolis, in 1987, had dropped to 356,677 people and it was expected to continually decline into the 1990s. But the seven-county Twin Cities area expanded to an estimated record of 2,254,500 people by 1987.

While the city lost population, it didn't lose its progress. The building boom also included the IDS tower and also City Center and Butler Square, both housing specialty stores and good restaurants, a new and ultra-modern Lutheran Brotherhood headquarters, a new Government Center and Orchestra Hall, home of the Minnesota Orchestra.

The city also advanced in culture. It had an excellent public library and two nationally-recognized art centers: the Minneapolis Institute of Art and Walker Art Center.

But it was the opening of the Guthrie Theater in 1963 that brought Minneapolis the most attention as a culture center in the Midwest. The fabled Children's Theatre soon was winning national awards, and the advent of the Guthrie also inspired a score of smaller legitimate theaters to be created or rejuvenated. Both professional and non-professional, they include Theatre in the Round, the Cricket, Mixed Blood Theater, Theatre de la Jeune Lune and At the Foot of the Mountain.

Minneapolis had come a long way since those pioneers settled to harvest the trees and produce flour. It had become a sophisticated and yet friendly city. It had grown in excellence and prospered. It had arrived.

Above: *A worker puts finishing touches on a Sixth Street Skyway in Minneapolis. An entire network of skyways allows people to go from building to building and not be outside. It's a winter blessing.*
Left: *City plows and other snow-removing equipment hit the streets of Minneapolis before snowstorms end. Here is a scene on Third Avenue Bridge over the Mississippi.*

Facing page: *Lake Street at sunset.*
STEVE SCHNEIDER PHOTOS

CHAPTER
4

St. Paul History

Above: *Henry Hastings Sibley helped organize Minnesota Territory and later became the first governor of the state of Minnesota.*

Right: *St. Paul's steamboat landing about 1900.* IMAGES COURTESY MINNESOTA HISTORICAL SOCIETY

He was a coarse, ill-looking, low-browed fellow, with only one eye, and that a sinister-looking one...Such was the man on whom Fortune, with that blind fatuity that seems to characterize the jade, thrust the honor of being the founder of our good city!

J. Fletcher Williams, *A History of the City of St. Paul*

He was Pierre "Pig's Eye" Parrant, a swarthy Canadian voyageur who illegally sold whisky to Indians and soldiers. In 1838, he settled into a log hut at Fountain Cave, near the present-day 35E bridge

From that hovel, he peddled his whisky to soldiers at Fort Snelling and to French trappers. His being near the

60

Mississippi allowed his customers to paddle their canoes right to his door. Parrant also diluted the whisky with water from the stream.

For many years, it was believed reluctantly that Parrant was the first to settle in what is now St. Paul. That was mainly because of Williams' 1876 history of St. Paul. Williams was secretary-librarian of the Minnesota Historical Society, which published his book. Of Parrant, he wrote:

"He, the immortal parent of our saintly city, and of the noble army of whisky-sellers who have thriven since that day—it, the first habitation, the first business-house, of our Christian metropolis of today! Thus was our city "founded"—by a pig-eyed retailer of whisky. The location of the future Capital of Minnesota was determined, not by the commanding and picturesque bluffs, a noble and inspiring site whereon to build a city—not by a great river flowing so majestically in front of it, suggestive of commerce and trade—but solely as a convenient spot to sell whisky, without the pale of law!"

Williams was a scholarly man, but not always accurate. Since his was the first major history of St. Paul, it was quoted by other historians for decades. Now, it is known from early maps that others—including Donald McDonald, Francis Desire and Joseph Turpin—settled in western St. Paul several years before "Pig's Eye" opened his saloon. But even today, many St. Paulites, when asked who was St. Paul's first resident, give the nod to "Pig's Eye."

As with Minneapolis, the first non-Indian to see what became St. Paul had been Father Louis Hennepin, the adventurous Franciscan. He was in a party of three that had been dispatched by LaSalle to explore the Mississippi as far north as possible in 1680.

Before he got too far, in the vicinity of Lake Pepin, he was captured by Sioux warriors. (Some historians say Hennepin may have joined the Indians willingly.) The Indians stripped Hennepin and his companions of their belongings, smashed their canoe and took them on foot to their village near Lake Mille Lac, about 90 miles north of the Twin Cities.

Hennepin and his party were "invited" to stay with the chief, Aquipaquetin, on an island. He did so until September of that year. About a month later, Hennepin discovered the Falls of St. Anthony.

The first birth of a white child and the first death to be recorded, the murder of a prominent man, occurred in 1839. On September 4, 1839, Basil Gervais was born. He was the son of Benjamin Gervais. It is interesting in light of today's feminism that the mother was listed only as Benjamin's wife.

Basil's parents were among a group of settlers, including Pig Eye Parrant, who had moved onto military land around Fountain Cave in 1839. They were forced to move out, and staked new claims around the lower steamboat landing. Parrant again set up a whisky shack. Later, when Parrant decided to move on, Benjamin Gervais bought his claim for $10—land that today is worth millions.

The first recorded death of a white man was the murder of John Hays in the fall of 1839. Someone bashed his head in and dumped his body near Carver's Cave. (Although he had a way with the Indians, Jonathan Carver's greatest historical claim was discovering, in terms of non-Indians, "The Great Cave." It was among St. Paul's most fascinating places. Later called "Carver's Cave," it was located in a sandstone area under what came to be known as Dayton's Bluff. Rock slides and and the advance of the railroads destroyed the cave's mouth.

Carver described the cave, which the Indians called "The Dwelling of the Great Spirit": "The bottom of it consists of fine, clear sand. About twenty feet from the en-

Today's Lowertown area, with Dayton's Bluff in the background.
COURTESY MINNESOTA HISTORICAL SOCIETY

Bridge Square, St. Paul, in 1871.
COURTESY MINNESOTA HISTORICAL SOCIETY

Suspicion in the death of John Hays immediately turned to Edward Phelan, whose land adjoined that of Hays.

Phelan was, in the eyes of the community, a hard, mean, unscrupulous man who often had argued with Hays. He is said to have replied to the question of how he and Hays got along as follows:

"Very badly. He is a lazy good-for-nothing. But never mind. I'll soon get rid of him."

He commonly was thought to be guilty, and was held at Prairie du Chien until his trial in the spring of 1840. Historian J. Fletcher Williams said Phelan must "stand, on the chronicles of our city, as its Cain—the first who inbrued his hands with the blood of his brother…"

However, Phelan was released for lack of evidence and later a disgruntled Sioux warrior claimed he had killed Hays. No motive has been recorded. The creek near St. Paul's Olympia Brewery named after Phelan is where he located his next claim. The differently spelled Lake Phalen also is named for him.

St. Paul, first named after wily "Pig's Eye," got its final title because of Father Lucien Galtier, a young French-Canadian priest, who came to the area in 1840. He was following parishioners from Mendota, where he had named his church for St. Peter. He named his new log church here for St. Paul. It was built on land donated by farmers Benjamin Gervais and Vetal Guerin.

The modest church, however, became the start of the culture of the city. Wrote Father Galtier:

"On the lst day of November [1841], I blessed the new basilica, and dedicated it to "St. Paul, the apostle of nations." I expressed a wish, at the same time, that the settlement would be known by the same name, and my desire was obtained."

Later, newspaper editor James Goodhue added:
"Pig's Eye, converted thou shalt be, like Saul;
"Arise, and be, henceforth, Saint Paul."

In the mid-19th century, St. Paul actually was two towns: Upper Landing and Lower Landing. They were separated by cleavage of the picturesque bluffs that dominated the area.

Mississippi steamboats came and went from Lower Landing, at the bottom of Jackson Street Upper Landing, the town beginning at the foot of Eagle and Chestnut Streets, served steamboats traveling the Minnesota River.

trance begins a lake, the water of which is transparent, and extends to an unsearchable distance; for the darkness of the cave prevents all attempts to acquire a knowledge of it. I threw a small pebble toward the interior parts of it with my utmost strength; I could hear that it fell into the water, and, notwithstanding it was of so small a size, it caused an agonizing and horrible noise, that reverberated through all those gloomy regions…"

"Life was not dull. When Vetal Guerin and Adele Perry were married in 1841, guests danced all night to Denis Cherrier's violin. Some days later, Guerin was leaning on his gatepost when a number of Indians, having passed several hours at Parrant's saloon, fired at him, the ball striking the post. Again, one morning Guerin opened his front door and an iron-headed arrow whizzed past him, striking the door jamb. Theirs was an eventful honeymoon."

Henry Jackson opened the first store in the area in 1842. He sold liquor and food and clothes and whatever. Later, he was appointed the first postmaster and created the first post office: a two-foot-square candle box.

Being a man of force and humor, Jackson easily attracted people to his store, not just to buy but to socialize. His place became a center for news and gossip and talk of politics.

Among his duties, Jackson was justice of the peace. His court was not always the scene of dignity and decorum. And then there was The Case of the Needed Violinist. He wasn't on trial, but was a member of a jury. The local constable had locked up the jury while it tried to reach a verdict.

A Stillwater man traveled to St. Paul to hire the violinist, believed to be one Charlie Mitchell. The fiddler was needed for a ball that evening. The Stillwater man was shocked to learn that Charlie was locked up.

Undaunted for long, he took a box to the window of the jury room, stood on it and engaged Charlie in conversation. Thinking this some kind of conspiracy, and possibly a bribe, other members of the jury objected.

A brawl ensued. They threw chairs and tables and wrestled each other to the floor. In the end, the place looked like a tornado had made a direct hit. Charlie had a dislocated arm, and two other jurors were badly bruised. The rest of the jury bolted and the case had to be dismissed. The ball was postponed.

Very slowly, St. Paul began to draw away from its rough, frontier life. Other merchants arrived and, by 1844, St. Paul had five stores, Father Galtier's log chapel and a tavern. Jacob Bass built the St. Paul House, the city's first hotel. And, in 1847, the first Sunday school was established. Seven children showed up, some speaking French, some English, some Sioux. Interpreters were needed.

They not only were divided by an 80′ bluff and swampy bottom land, but also had their own residential and business communities. There was intense rivalry between them. Although there were a few American families living in the area, most were French Canadians and Swiss. English was the language of only a few residents.

Housing was mainly primitive log cabins with furniture made of split timber. Clay and marsh hay made the cement. Life could be dangerous. Virginia Brainard Kunz, in her book, *St. Paul: Saga of an American City,* describes a typical scene:

By 1844, St. Paul boasted five stores, Father Galtier's log chapel and a tavern.

Left: *Father Lucien Galtier, who arrived here in 1840, is responsible for St. Paul's name.* COURTESY MINNESOTA HISTORICAL SOCIETY

A muddy, rutted Third Street in the early 1870s, looking east from Market Street. ILLINGWORTH PHOTO COURTESY MINNESOTA HISTORICAL SOCIETY

Long awaited were school teachers. The leaders of the settlers knew that, if St. Paul were to become a major city, it would need education for their children.

So, Mrs. Matilda Rumsey got a warm reception when she arrived in 1845. She was to stay only a few months, but she opened the first school in a log structure in the vicinity of Upper Landing. Two years later, Harriet Bishop arrived from Vermont and became St. Paul's first permanent teacher. Author Kunz tells of her:

"Harriet Bishop was a remarkable woman. She once described herself, with a typically Victorian flourish, as a 'feeble and timid young lady. but she apparently was neither. According to T.M. Newson, an early St. Paul editor, she was 'angular, positive, determined—such a woman as is necessary for frontier life…tall, with a good figure; a bright, expressive face; earnest and decided in manners, and quick in speech'."

Because of river transportation, St. Paul became the fur-trading center of the Northwest. Pelts were brought in by ox cart from the Red River region and shipped off on steamboats.

Fur trading brought in only $1,400 in 1844, but it grew steadily to more than $182,000 in 1857 and to $250,000 in 1863. It eventually became a million-dollar industry for the St. Paul merchants—at a time when a million dollars was an incredible amount of money.

One of the most significant events was the creation of Minnesota Territory on March 3, 1849, and the naming of St. Paul as its capital. Within weeks, construction of 70 new buildings had begun. People began flowing into the new capital. The population reached 910 by the 1850 census.

An indication of the growth of the city is found in the first business directory, published in 1850 by the *Minnesota Pioneer,* first newspaper of the territory. Among its entries: 14 lawyers, two blacksmiths, five clergymen, 16 stores, five masons, 18 carpenters, four doctors and a shoemaker.

No town can be established without a shoot-out. One of sorts took place in 1854. It seems that James Goodhue, editor of the *Pioneer,* took on Judge David Cooper in print. Among other things, he called the judge a brute, a sot, an ass and a "profligate vagabond," and accused him of playing cards on Sunday.

Goodhue included others in his diatribe and ended with: "…we sat down to write this article with some bitterness, but our very gall is honey to what they deserve."

Joseph Cooper, the judge's brother, was livid. They met the next day on the street, and Cooper told Goodhue he would "blow your [expletive] brains out."

They both drew pistols, and the sheriff promptly stepped in and disarmed them. Or thought he did. Cooper had a knife which he stuck into Goodhue's stomach. Then editor Goodhue pulled a second pistol and shot Cooper, "inflicting a very serious wound on him." It was not reported where the bullet went into Cooper's body.

Cooper, still upright, rushed at Goodhue and stabbed him again, this time in the back. They were sepa-

rated and hauled away. They both survived, and St. Paul had something to talk about for months.

As with most frontier towns, St. Paul still was somewhat uncivilized. But, despite the brawling and lack of good law enforcement, there was an element of the town that worked hard, went to church and brought a sense of order to the community.

St. Paul might not be the state capital today had it not been for Joe Rolette, a colorful legislator and fur trader known to affect Indian dress. He was brilliant and enjoyed a bit of skullduggery now and then.

Rolette came to St. Paul's rescue in 1857 after the territorial legislature passed a bill to relocate the capital to St. Peter, Minn. All the bill needed was the governor's signature.

Although he was the representative from Pembina, in what would become North Dakota, Rolette liked St. Paulites. When the bill got to him as chairman of the enrollment committee, he locked it in a bank vault and, for five days, disappeared. Reports falsely indicated he was heading north on a dog sled.

Just as the legislative session ended, Rolette reappeared. Another copy of the bill, signed by territorial governor Willis Gorman, later was struck down in court.

The late 1850s were vital to the progress of St. Paul. Minnesota became the 32nd state on May 11, 1858, and, in 1859, grain was exported for the first time.

But things went sour in 1859. State-backed bonds worth $5 million, issued to build badly-needed railroads despite the national depression that followed the Panic of

Above: *The northwest corner of Third and Wabasha streets in 1887.* ARTHUR C. WARNER PHOTO COURTESY MINNESOTA HISTORICAL SOCIETY

Left: *The Hon. Joe Rolette, 1856. He saw to it that St. Paul stayed Minnesota's capital.* COURTESY MINNESOTA HISTORICAL SOCIETY

1857, became worthless without a foot of track being laid. Gov. Henry Sibley had to call out the militia to control frontier lawlessness.

St. Paul that year had its own scandal: the murder of Stanislaus Bilanski, a moody, cantankerous, tyrannical, jealous saloonkeeper. He was thought to have died of acute indigestion, but later suspicion centered on his wife, Ann Wright Bilanski. In his book, *Murder in Minnesota,* Walter Trenerry, describes the public's interest in the case:

"Its fascination was irresistible, for when a lovely woman stoops to folly she is not likely to do it halfheartedly. Throwing her cap over the moon, she follows where passion leads her and all the world enjoys watching."

The wife might have gotten away with it, except for an attack of conscience by a woman friend. The friend finally confessed that she had accompanied Ann Bilanski to a store to buy arsenic.

Ann Bilanski was charged with first degree murder. It was revealed she was having an affair with a young lodger, John Walker. Walker denied it all, claiming Ann Bilanski actually was his aunt.

The newspapers, as was their practice in those days, moralized freely. In an editorial, the *Pioneer and Democrat* commented on the case:

"It was the repetition of a tragedy, which has been enacted all the world over, wherever a woman, bad enough to be a harlot and bold enough to be a murderer, has wished to get rid of a husband whom she disliked, for a paramour whom she preferred."

Ann Bilanski was found guilty and sentenced to be hanged. St. Paulites loved the scandal, but hanging a woman was another matter. Never had a woman been executed in the state. Governor Sibley was confronted by protests and even threats. The Legislature considered abolishing capital punishment, but later decided to keep it.

Sibley stalled until his term was up and his successor, Alexander Ramsey, got the intensely political issue. He finally ordered Ann Bilanski hanged "between the hours of 10:00 a.m. and 2:00 p.m. on Friday, March 23, 1860." His decision caused a renewed uproar, but to no avail.

About 1,500 people showed up for the hanging. Author Trenerry reports the address of the first Minnesota woman to be executed:

"I die without having had any mercy shown me, or justice. I die for the good of my soul, and not for murder.

In 1888, 12 railroads served 8 million passengers at the St. Paul Union Depot

May you all profit by my death. Your courts of justice are not courts of justice—but I will get justice in Heaven. I am a guilty woman, I know, but not of this murder, which was committed by another. I forgive everybody who did me wrong. I die a sacrifice to the law…"

The Civil War, as tragic as it was, helped to unify St. Paul. The first man in the union to be mustered in to fight the South was a St. Paulite: Josias R. King. He was a member of St. Paul's Pioneer Guard, which became the First Minnesota Infantry Regiment immediately after the surrender of Fort Sumter. In all, 1,498 men out of the city's population of about 11,000 joined the Union Army. One hundred and twenty-four died in the war. Among them was Gen. Alexander Wilkin, who had settled in St. Paul in 1849. He was killed at the Battle of Tupelo.

Following the war was a period of prosperity and the railroad era was underway. From a 10-mile stretch of the St. Paul and Pacific Railroad from St. Paul to St. Anthony, the railroad industry blossomed over 30 years to a nationwide network spreading from the Saintly City. Twelve rail lines were built, including the Great Northern, Northern Pacific, the Chicago, St. Paul, Minneapolis and Omaha, the Wisconsin Central and the Soo Line. Eight million passengers used the St. Paul Union Depot in 1888.

Meanwhile, the city was changing radically. The railroads destroyed some lovely neighborhoods, changing them to industrial areas. Old wooden buildings, some of which were victims of fire, were replaced with sturdy limestone and brick structures. Meeting halls and theaters were built, and the residents were most proud of the St. Paul

Left and facing page: *St. Paul's busy Union Depot yards in 1918 and today.* LEFT: STEVE SCHNEIDER; FACING PAGE, COURTESY MINNESOTA HISTORICAL SOCIETY

67

A postcard view of the Ice Palace at the 1916 revival of the St. Paul Winter Carnival. COURTESY MINNESOTA HISTORICAL SOCIETY

Opera House, which housed everything from the St. Paul Musical Society orchestra to cancan dancers from Paris.

Sixth and Seventh Streets became the center of the downtown area and the city's first Chamber of Commerce was formed. In 1889, the Pioneer Building was constructed—becoming the city's first skyscraper—all of 12 stories high.

The notorious Younger brothers, James and Cole, added to the flavor of the city. In 1901, they got out of Stillwater Prison, conditionally pardoned for the 1876 Northfield bank robbery, and headed for St. Paul. Cole started selling tombstones and James, reportedly thwarted in his efforts to marry a St. Paul woman or find lawful employment, killed himself in a St. Paul hotel.

In the early 20th century, the people of St. Paul wanted a peaceful, recreational city. They wanted family unity and some places where their children could play. The political leaders took note and, by 1912, there were 12 playgrounds.

Four years later, the St. Paul Winter Carnival was revived. It had been created in 1886 to prove to the world that one can live during the winter in Minnesota, but hardly had become an annual event (which wouldn't happen till 1937, with a WWII hiatus). Often a main feature of the carnival is the Ice Palace, which has been touted nationally as a rare feat of architecture.

King Boreas, usually a St. Paul businessman, rules over the carnival until dethroned by Vulcan, the fire devil. It's all fun and games with grownups being sillier than unbridled school boys.

The carnival spirit was interrupted by World War I. A swirl of patriotism engulfed St. Paul. People put up with food shortages cheerfully. Because wheat was scarce, women baked their bread with rye or potato flour or barley. Women made surgical dressings, and canned a lot of food, and men learned to fix their own cars.

The young men went into service. An ambulance unit from St. Paul's Hamline University was the first to leave the state after the U.S. entered the war. A Home Guard was formed to replace the National Guardsmen who left for active service. The 400 members checked men in pool halls, saloons and the like to see if they had their draft registration cards. They also were called in to quell disturbances such as the October 1917 streetcar strike. They kept order. As true descendants of pioneers, the St. Paulites survived the war and turned to more constructive things.

The image of women as dainty, fragile creatures in lace who were capable of little more than powdering their noses and giggling didn't fit St. Paul women at all. They got involved. As Virginia Brainard Kunz reported:

"St. Paul's women organized Children's Health Days, opened milk stations in schools to provide children with free milk, formed Mothers' Clubs that grew into Parent-Teacher Associations, taught Americanization classes, established more than thirty public drinking fountains throughout the city, and organized classes to teach the needy how to sew their own clothing.

"Some of their activities were surprisingly contemporary. They worked for prison reform and freedom for political prisoners, promoted the beautification of the city through the planting of trees and shrubbery, protested the high cost of living and sought solutions for it, worked for highway improvements, opposed the death penalty, supported indeterminate sentencing, and backed a Duluth-St. Lawrence Seaway—all before 1920."

The man who introduced the Prohibition amendment, Andrew Volstead, a Minnesota Congressman, maintained his office in St. Paul. His home base responded to Prohibition like the rest of the nation. Scores of speakeasies spouted in town and St. Paulites displayed their ability to have a good time.

In one day of 1923, almost 100 bootleggers were arraigned in St. Paul's Federal District Court. Even a soft drink bar on Cedar Street went to hard liquor. On April 25, 1927, two men and a woman were slain near the capitol. They were in the illegal liquor business.

St. Paul became a haven for gangsters. When things got hot in other cities, they would come to rest in St. Paul. Among the "vacationers" were Kate (Ma) Barker, Alvin Karpis, Homer Van Meter, Baby Face Nelson and the most famous of them all: John Dillinger.

For the most part, they did not practice their trade in St. Paul. The idea was to rest, not to commit crimes. The police knew they were about, but laid off. One reason was that, when an amateur robber started working in the city, the big-time gangsters would see him out of town. They wanted no trouble.

The *St. Paul Pioneer Press* once demanded to know why the gangsters such as Dillinger "have chosen St. Paul as their hideaway while the police and federal agents were scouring the nation for them." In defense of his force, Police Chief Thomas Dahill replied: "Dillinger is better armed than the entire police force."

Dillinger's rest was interrupted in 1934. A city detective and a federal agent knocked on the door of the gangster's St. Paul apartment. Dillinger greeted them by firing his submachine gun through the door. The officers fled and Dillinger escaped.

St. Paul's truce with visiting gangsters ended when the Barker-Karpis gang broke the rules, resulting in the city's two most famous kidnappings. In 1933, they grabbed William Hamm, Jr., prestigious St. Paul brewery owner, off a St. Paul street and demanded $100,000 ransom. The money was paid and Hamm was released near Wyoming, Minn. No one was caught.

Then, in 1934, the same gang kidnapped Edward Bremer, a St. Paul banker, as he was driving to work. Ma Barker decided that inflation demanded $200,000. She got

St. Paul in the Prohibition Era became a vacation spot for gangsters, including John Dillinger

the money and Bremer was let go, unharmed, in St. Paul's west end.

Two years later, Karpis was captured in New Orleans and returned to St. Paul, where he was tried for crimes other than the kidnappings. He was convicted and sent to prison.

It had been a dismal period for St. Paulites—Prohibition with its gangsters and the Depression with its auster-

Above left: *Andrew Volstead, the Congressman from St. Paul who introduced the Prohibition amendment.* COURTESY MINNESOTA HISTORICAL SOCIETY

69

Right: *A view from a stereopticon that card recorded the facade of the St. Paul Opera House.*
Facing page: *Plowing out the Anoka area north of Minneapolis after 1940's Armistice Day blizzard.*
PHOTOS COURTESY MINNESOTA HISTORICAL SOCIETY

ity. In 1933, St. Paul was where some 20,000 farmers gathered to ask the state legislature for financial help. They wanted tax relief and aid for debtors. In the city, people were paid $1 a day to work on the streets and in the parks. Some people took jobs that paid in groceries.

One bright spot in that period was the appearance of Eleanor Roosevelt in 1939. She opened the Women's Institute of St. Paul, at a meeting attended by about 12,000 women. Surviving until after World War II, the institute would bring speakers to the city and would build the women's City Club (now part of the Minnesota Museum of Art).

Hardly had St. Paulites settled down after Prohibition and the Depression when Mother Nature shook them badly. It was called the Armistice Day Storm of 1940. It was the most devastating November snow storm in the history of the region.

November normally was much too early for such a storm, and the Twin Cities, particularly St. Paul, were not prepared. The city snowplows still were in *mothballs*. Trolleys became marooned throughout the city and some 2,000 cars were snowbound on downtown streets.

You couldn't get a hotel room if you were the mayor, and cots were brought out in office buildings.

The "storm" in Europe also began to affect St. Paul that November, even with U.S. involvement following Pearl Harbor more than a year away. Drafting of men began, and the 18th Infantry Battalion was activated in St. Paul. The Marine Reserve ground unit was dispatched to Camp Elliott, California, and later to Iceland.

The "Yellow Perils," biplane trainers of the Navy and Marine Air Reserve, began flying near the city. And coastal defenses were beefed up by activating St. Paul's 206th Infantry Regiment.

But, like Minneapolis, most of St. Paul was isolated from the eventual war. The people learned to live with goods rationing and frozen wages and prices. The main complaint was gasoline rationing. Midwesterners, with the wide-open spaces and easily accessible cities, generally drove their own cars to work. Now it was streetcars—300 were added to St. Paul's barn—and buses and a deluge of grumbling.

There were St. Paulites who lost loved ones in the war, and those whose loved ones came home maimed. But they were in the minority and St. Paul was safe. Some city leaders began shouting wolf, and some air raid shelters were built. They were mostly laughed at.

Although St. Paul men went to war, St. Paul experienced a population increase. In 1942, population was 297,781, or 7,500 more than when the war began. Many St. Paul men married while in the service and had children. When the war ended, and the servicepeople came home, the migration to the suburbs began. Within 15 years, St. Paul suburbs doubled, tripled or quadrupled.

As in Minneapolis, the flow to the suburbs left St. Paul with families who couldn't afford to leave town and a downtown that lost shoppers to the suburban malls. In the 1950s and 1960s, there was an urge to tear down urban buildings and houses. The city appeared to be dying.

But in the 1970s, public and private leaders and organization decided to turn it all around. And, like the phoenix, St. Paul arose from the ashes. There was much new construction and restoration, including the historic Landmark Center in the heart of downtown. The Ordway Music Theater, one of the finest in the nation, and the World Trade Center gave St. Paul an international reputation.

By 1985, St. Paul was alive. It had received an All-American City title and a Livability Award. It was a showplace, a city to be reckoned with, a city the saints could admire.

70

CHAPTER 5

ECONOMY OF THE TWIN CITIES

Above: *At the Minnesota State Fair, St. Paul.*
Right: *Straight lines, glass and steel are common ingredients of the newer downtown St. Paul buildings.*
STEVE SCHNEIDER PHOTOS

As much wisdom may be expended on a private economy as on an empire, and as much wisdom may be drawn from it.

Emerson, *Essays, First Series: Prudence*

A St. Paul street scene: a constrast of small-town atmosphere and big-city bustle. STEVE SCHNEIDER

The early entrepreneurs of the Twin Cities deserve little credit for creating the area's first major industry: lumbering. After all, when they began operations in the 1830s, some 70 percent of Minnesota was blanketed with trees.

Before lumbering diminished, flour milling began. The state's population, from 1850 to 1860, took off like a souped-up space shuttle. In those years, it rose from 6,000 to 172,000 people. More than 90 percent of these migrants settled in rural areas, many establishing grain farms. Flour milling was a natural. It didn't take a Ph.D. from Harvard Business School to figure that out.

But credit should go to those who followed. Both lumbering and milling faded as the area's top businesses, beginning about 1900. But there were new industries created to take their places, and new ones to take the place of those ventures.

When needed, new ideas for development came forth. Thus, jobs and prosperity and growth continued.

Why such a record? It's the people. The Twin Cities economy began with a breed of hard-working, mostly well-educated entrepreneurs, many from New England, who wanted the area to succeed. They were not against making their own fortunes, however.

And, unlike in many cities, the Twin Citians formed a close society. In his book, *The M-Form Society: How American Teamwork Can Recapture the Competitive Edge,* William G. Ouchi describes the closeness in Minneapolis, which also abounds in St. Paul:

"What is remarkable is that Minneapolis is a community. It is a community of people who are connected to one another, who place peer pressure on one another, who remember for fifty or one hundred years who has been helpful and who has not. Like any community it can at times be forceful, perhaps even heavy-handed in insisting on local values, but, on the whole, it succeeds by not diminishing individualism, but by creating a balanced environment in which entrepreneurs like the maverick Bill Norris can build companies [Control Data] and create visions....These individualists, rather than being narrow-minded profit seekers at odds with their environment and adversaries of their city, become part of the community."

As early as the 1850s, there was evidence of diversification in the Twin Cities. It wasn't much by today's standards, but, in 1854, Orrin Rogers started a sash and door factory in Minneapolis. A year later, a factory to make tools for the lumbering industry was opened and, in 1857, H.C. Butler started making manufacturing tools.

The first national bank in the area was created in 1872. The millers needed large amounts of cash in the fall to buy wheat from farmers, but the flour wasn't sold until the next year. During the rest of the year, the millers needed money for normal operations.

Out-of-state banks took to this feast-or-famine credit situation with all the enthusiasm of a duck anticipating

hunting season. So, in typical Minnesota pioneer fashion, the millers started their own national bank, Northwestern National Bank.

Next came the problem of rail transportation. The millers desperately needed access to the east-coast seaports. But the existing railroads tied the northwest farm area only to Chicago and Milwaukee. Also, there was a need to ship grain from the west, as far as the Dakotas, eastward.

Again the millers stood up to the challenge: they built their own railroad. It was called the Minneapolis, St. Paul and Sault Ste. Marie. The new line ran from the Twin Cities to Sault Ste. Marie, the junction of Lakes: Superior and Huron.

Dubbed the Soo Line, the railway connected the Twin Cities with the Canadian Pacific Railroad, which opened up the markets in Montreal and Boston. Take that Chicago and Milwaukee. A year after the Soo Line was finished in 1887, it was delivering more wheat to the east than any other railway.

Using technological developments, the millers began producing huge amounts of flour products and they badly needed to expand their markets. In his book, *City of Lakes: An Illustrated History of Minneapolis,* Joseph Stepanovich describes the solution:

"Intensive merchandising of their products at home and abroad was the essence of the milling interests' new activity. To develop the national market, the various milling companies hired specialists in retail trade and advertising to complement their corporate staffs. The most successful of these individuals was James S. Bell, who joined Washburn Crosby Company [the father of General Mills] in 1888. At the same time, William H. Dunwoody journeyed to London for an extended stay to help establish markets for flour and Upper Midwestern grain in Europe. The efforts paid handsome dividends in a relatively short period of time and, by the end of the 1890s, Minneapolis was the flour-milling center of the United States and of the world." No matter what they needed these early entrepreneurs found a way to obtain it.

While Minneapolis was obsessed with its wheat-flour business, St. Paul was developing its wholesale and retail trade. It dominated those businesses in Minnesota during the 1870s, far surpassing the efforts in Minneapolis. St. Paul wholesalers alone sold more than $27 million worth of goods by 1877. Minneapolis wholesalers racked up only $8 million in sales.

It was inevitable that the Twin Cities would become a significant insurance center. A lot was invested in machinery, equipment and business property.

And the farmers were clamoring for life insurance. Taking an early lead was Northwestern National Life Insurance Co., which opened in Minneapolis in 1885. The company still is a dominant factor in the Twin Cities insurance complex. Also important was St. Paul Fire and Marine Insurance Company, founded in 1853, the oldest business corporation in Minnesota. It is now the St. Paul Companies, Inc.

The birth of high tech in the area can be traced to a shy, quiet man named Al Butz. In 1883, he was proprietor of a run-down company that made fire extinguishers. On the side, Butz was a would-be inventor. He liked to work up new gimmicks and was fascinated by heating problems.

In 1885, Butz created a much-needed device: a "damper flapper" that automatically controlled fires in furnaces and boilers. He rented a shed in Minneapolis and formed the Consolidated Temperature Controlling Company. One of his $1,500 investors was William R. Sweatt, board chairman of something called Honeywell Heating Specialties Company.

In 1927, Butz and Sweatt merged their companies and, thus was born Honeywell, now a world-wide giant in high-tech industries.

St. Paul's early economic history had begun with the region's first international dealers: the French and British fur traders. The furs they obtained from Indian hunters were shipped down the Mississippi River and ultimately to the East and Europe.

It was the Mississippi that made St. Paul a transportation center, first with steamboats and other river craft in the 1840s and then with railroads. The railway industry in St. Paul was born in 1861 when the city's first locomotive, the *William Crooks,* arrived.

Led by James J. Hill, the city became a regional rail center by the end of the 19th century. Aside from Hill's Great Northern, there were 11 other lines going in and out of the city. Some 150 trains used the St. Paul Union Depot every day.

As the 19th century came to a close, Twin Cities business leaders began taking a deep interest in the University of Minnesota, until then an institution devoted to Aristotle and Shakespeare and Michelangelo.

The business community wanted more emphasis on science and engineering. John S. Pillsbury, of the famed milling family, donated funds for the construction of Pillsbury Hall on campus. There was one requirement: the building had to be used for scientific research. The university board of regents in that era always had milling men among its members.

Soon, the university became most important to the economic welfare of the region. As Joseph Stepanovich writes:

"The university's role grew more and more important as the 20th century rolled along, for basic research and experimentation grew more complex and costly as time went by. It is not too strong a judgment to conclude that industry, agriculture, and mining in the state could not have progressed as they have without the beneficial activities of the faculty of the University of Minnesota."

Despite the automobile age, the Twin Cities had electric street cars until the 1950s. The clanging trolleys carried 140 million passengers in the 1920s and people loved the ride. It was another factor in forming a community. A trolley ride often became a social event. People got engaged on streetcars, and some made the decision to get divorced on them.

The early and mid-20th century saw Twin Citians survive World War I and Prohibition and the Depression and World War II. Business leaders kept cool when things were tough, and seized opportunities during good times.

It was the second world war that revived prosperity for the cities. Onan Corporation managed to produce most of the electrical power plants for the armed services. Munsingwear and other clothing manufacturers made blankets, underwear and other garment needs for the war. Pillsbury and General Mills got into food products for the troops. And so it went.

The population benefited from the war, as employment rose sharply and people had money to spend. They could go out to eat, and the restaurant business boomed. They could go to movies and the theater, and those industries took off.

By mid-century, the Twin Cities were established as an important economic center and had won the respect of business and industry leaders throughout the world.

The Twin Cities economy began with a breed of hard-working, well educated entrepreneurs

Facing page: *In downtown Minneapolis, a street musician escapes the winter cold in a skyway.*
STEVE SCHNEIDER

The Twin Cities Economy Today

There are 16 Twin Cities companies on *Fortune's* list of the 500 largest industrial corporations in America. Among them 3M Company, 39th on the list; Honeywell, Inc., 52nd; Pillsbury Company, 61st; and General Mills, 80th.

Besides 3M, the three top St. Paul area firms on the list are Land O'Lakes, Inc., 164th; Farmers Union Central Exchange, 260th; and Ecolab, 352nd.

On the *Fortune* list of the 100 largest diversified service firms, Super Valu Stores is first. TCF Banking and Savings is 19th on the list of the 50 largest savings institutions and Dayton Hudson Corporation is 11th among the 50 biggest retailing firms. There are 10 other Twin Cities firms on the *Fortune* service company list, including Minnesota Mutual Life Insurance Co. of St. Paul.

It is a sign of the strong, diversified economy of the cities, which includes electronics, medical products, machinery, milling, food processing and a huge printing industry.

In revenue, the largest company in the area is a private one: Cargill. The firm, which started as one small town grain elevator and since has diversified, has 323 companies in 55 countries throughout the world. Its yearly revenues exceed $30 billion.

What makes the Twin Cities so special? The Greater Minneapolis Chamber of Commerce, in a 1987 booklet, *Economic Profile,* gives reasons for the development of the area. Here are some of them:

- Major business strengths include: a highly-educated work force; access to high technology; excellent transportation services; low-cost energy and available capital.
- The University of Minnesota, with its main campuses in the Twin Cities, is a major research institution. Its nearly 45,000 full-time students earn degrees in 250 fields of study. Former students and faculty have been awarded 12 Nobel Prizes for physics, medicine, chemistry, economics, and peace.
- Of people 25 years old or older in the Minneapolis-St. Paul area, 80 percent are high school graduates and 22 percent have 16 years of education or more. The high school graduation rate in Minnesota is the highest in the nation.

- Income is higher than most metropolitan areas. The 1984 median income for all families in the seven-county metropolitan area was $32,297, as compared to the national figure of $26,433.

R.T. Rybak, of the Downtown Council in Minneapolis, said the Twin Cities economy directly affects a five-state area in the Midwest. And it's expanding.

"It can be argued that we have made inroads in Detroit, for instance," reports Rybak. "Republic Airlines [now merged with Northwest Airlines] was strong in Detroit. And Dayton Hudson has been active there. It seems we are establishing ourselves, outside of Chicago, as the economic center of the upper central states."

A University of Minnesota economist maintains you cannot separate the economy of Minneapolis from that of St. Paul. "It is definitely a metro area economy," said Wilbur Maki, who has done extensive research on the subject.

Above: *The Vulcans, those who would destroy winter, march during the St. Paul Winter Carnival.*

Facing page: *A St. Paul neighborhood scene, highlighted by one of the city's many churches.*
STEVE SCHNEIDER PHOTOS

Maki is intrigued with a fairly new industry in the area: the manufacturing of products that don't go to the consumer, but are used in production of other products.

"That's very much the situation in electronics. It's a big thing here. The Twin Cities is one of a half-dozen places with a combination of finances, education, research and development, manufacturing and services that support technological innovation. It's not surprising we are going through a period of unprecedented overall growth."

The educator contends another growth market ripe for the Twin Cities is in environmental controls.

"There is a tremendous interest in it, a demand for it all over the world. To the extent we get into that area, it will generate an uplift in the economy."

Some other Maki observations:

- There is a very high level of entrepreneurship in the metro area. A lot of venture capital is available. We have more venture financing than we have good products to finance.
- Why is entrepreneurship so high? Partly, it's exposure to ideas. We are a tremendous communications center, a huge knowledge transfer center. We have a highly-interactive society.
- The area has the potential to expand. We don't have the environmental problems of some cities. There will be 20 [U.S.] cities who face severe environment problems by the year 2,000. We don't fall into that category.
- We are much more dependent on world trade in this area than in many others. We need to develop a lot more market intelligence about world trade, particularly world trade opportunities for small businesses. They need to expand internationally.

In 1987, the $120 million Minnesota World Trade Center was opened in downtown St. Paul. It is hoped to be a significant factor in the promotion of world trade.

There is optimism in the Twin Cities about its economic future. If the tradition of creativity and imagination continues, there is good reason for that optimism.

Community Involvement

It has long been a tradition in the Twin Cities area for corporations to give of their time and money for a better life in the community.

That began with the pioneer entrepreneurs, such as the Washburns and Crosbys and James J. Hill, who, after

accumulating wealth, gave some of it back to the people.

And the tradition is not confined to doling out money. Business executives regularly serve on boards of civic and charity and arts organizations. Others before them did it. It is expected of them and they comply.

Sandra Scott, assistant manager for research of the Greater Minneapolis Chamber of Commerce, puts it this way:

"We have a reputation for civic responsibility. You don't just come to work and get a paycheck and go home. You are expected to help in our society.

"On a per capita basis, we have more non-profit arts activities than New York City."

Sarah Dreiling, community affairs director for the St. Paul Chamber of Commerce, spoke for St. Paul firms: "The St. Paul business community has a long-standing history of

Above: *The landscaped beauty of the University of Minnesota campus.*
Left: *The University of Minnesota is important to community health care as well as the general economy.*
Facing page: *An interior view of Riverplace.* STEVE SCHNEIDER PHOTOS

79

 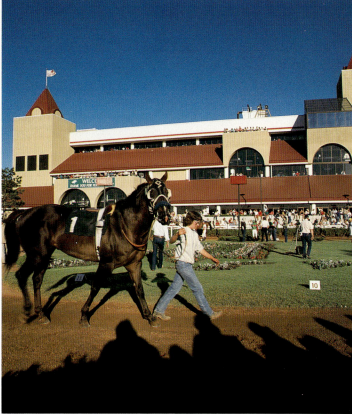

Above: *Skateboard competition during the Minneapolis Aquatennial.* **Right:** *St. Paul's Canterbury Downs.*

Facing page: *A scene at Minneapolis-St. Paul International Airport. Becoming an airline hub has greatly enhanced Twin Cities businesses.*
STEVE SCHNEIDER PHOTOS

responsiveness to community and citizens' needs. They have demonstrated a caring for the quality of life in St. Paul.

"The business people have trained leaders of community organizations, taken part in community affairs and community issues and formed a business-education partnership to sponsor programs in St. Paul public schools.

Sixty-two firms, in Minneapolis alone, gave five percent of pretax profits to charity. The Two Percent Club, firms that give two percent of pretax profits, has 21 members.

With his wife, Maude, William McKnight formed the McKnight Foundation in 1953—an organization that yearly gives away tens of millions of dollars to worthy projects. It funds everything from neighborhood self-help programs to health care to the arts in the Twin Cities. Another 3M executive, Archibald Bush, and his family created the Bush Foundation in St. Paul, a multimillion-dollar organization. Among other things, it funds a Leadership Program, a project to let already-established people take a leave and go back to school. The idea is to prepare them for greater leadership.

The fiscal year 1979-1980 saw Minnesota businesses and foundations give a total of $112 million back to communities where they operate. Fifty-eight percent went to the Twin Cities area.

A large amount of the money comes from large corporations. But not all are large. Others who contribute regularly include Anderson's China Shop, Creative Printing and Harold Chevrolet.

Usually, a firm makes its own decision as to where the money goes. So far, more than 40 percent has gone to health and welfare and about 24 percent to education.

William G. Ouchi, author of *The M-Form Society*, describes the phenomenon in Minneapolis (it also applies to St. Paul):

"Some might argue that publicly-owned businesses should not give to charity at all, that instead they should return dividends to shareholders, each of whom can choose the charity he or she prefers. In essence, the logic of free choice underlying such an argument is unassailable. The fact, however, is that each of us benefits through a healthy community and, in Minneapolis, that community is sustained largely through corporate giving. The pattern of corporate giving in Minneapolis makes it clear that the corporate decision-makers are small enough in number and tied closely enough together to comprise a community with a memory."

Here are the stories of five of the Twin Cities' largest and most influential firms:

Cargill

At the age of 21, William Wallace Cargill left his small farm home in Janesville, Wisconsin, to make a mark in the world. He had little thought then of becoming the founder of one of the nation's biggest private companies.

Cargill was the son of a Scottish sea captain, William Dick Cargill, who sailed from Scotland to New York City in 1838. The captain was a shrewd man who wanted to invest in shipping and trading.

His success was such that, in 1857, he sold his interests, moved the family to Janesville and retired on the farm.

Young Cargill, the third of six children, boarded a train without a clear idea of what he might do. He had some idea of buying a farm of his own.

He rode the train until it ran out of track: at Conover, a small town in northeastern Iowa. He could not afford the prices asked for farmland then, so he went to work at a menial task—stacking grain bags in a flathouse.

The young Scot worked hard and used the shrewdness he had inherited from the captain. Soon, he became a partner in the grain company. And not long after that, he owned it all. He called it the Cargill Elevator Co.

Cargill kept close track of the expanding railroads in Midwest farm states. As the railroads grew, so did Cargill Elevator, which soon needed a larger headquarters town. Cargill moved into Minnesota temporarily, first at Austin and then Albert Lea, then to LaCrosse, Wisconsin.

Enter another Scottish family: the MacMillans. While in LaCrosse in the 1880s, the MacMillans invested in Cargill Elevator. In 1895, the relationship was firmed when Cargill's daughter, Edna, married John H. MacMillan, son of Duncan D. MacMillan, a businessman and lawyer. Offspring of both families hold executive positions today. Since 1977, Whitney MacMillan, great-grandson of Duncan, has been chairman of the company.

Cargill Elevator headquarters was moved to Minneapolis in 1884 and, in 1946, to the Minneapolis suburb of Minnetonka.

The Cargill-MacMillans believed in plowing profits back into the business. They also didn't want just ownership. They wanted to become part of the operation and they did.

Until 1945, the firm handled grain and commodity transactions almost exclusively. Now it is a true conglomerate. Here are just a few of the company's activities, aside from grain and commodities:

- Financial services. This includes financial-instrument merchandising, foreign-exchange management investments and equipment leasing.
- Milling and processing. The firm operates plants that process soybeans and other oilseeds in the United States and eight other countries throughout the world. It processes other products in plants around the globe.
- Research. Cargill is deeply involved in research of hybrid corn, wheat, sorghum and sunflower seeds. It also produces and markets such products.

Cargill has 28,000 employees in the U.S. and another 18,000 in other parts of the world. It has 323 companies in 55 countries. It operates a private internal communications system and spends about $50 million on year just keeping in touch with everything. Dollar sales exceed $30 billion.

And all because a 21-year-old son of a Scottish sea captain wanted to make something of himself.

3M Company

The fact that 3M exists is somewhat of a business miracle. It was formed in 1902 by a group of businessmen in Two Harbors, Minn., a quaint little town on the North

Shore of Lake Superior. It appeared to be run by the likes of Laurel and Hardy.

The founders figured they'd get rich via an inferior mineral they thought was corundum—a hard mineral containing abrasive qualities useful to grinding wheel manufacturers. The mineral turned out to be worthless.

So, tail between legs, the company limped on down to Duluth and started making sandpaper. Again, failure.

This time the company moved to St. Paul. There was some improvement in the product and the owners got the idea they should have salesmen. But it took a sales boom caused by World War I to establish the company as a going concern.

In the 1920s, the firm developed a waterproof sandpaper and the first masking tape. And then the big one: Scotch Brand transparent tape. This was followed by reflective road-sign material, magnetic recording tape, Thermo-Fax office copiers and other inventions.

In 1931, sales reached $4.67 million. Twenty years later sales had soared to $170 million. In recent years, 3M revenues were more than $7 billion.

The firm's success can be traced to the encouragement of creative inventions, and a lot of hard work by its very loyal employees. 3M also is an organization with a constant eye to the future—no resting on past successes. Now headquartered in Maplewood, a suburb east of St. Paul, the company operates in 49 countries of the world.

A lot of the credit goes to a man who joined the firm in 1907 as a bookkeeper. The late William L. McKnight was a practical person, down-to-earth and very brilliant. He was staunchly for free enterprise, but he avoided politics as if it was a frenzied skunk.

McKnight often was quoted as saying: "You must sleep, eat and work 3M or you won't get hired." If you show such devotion to the company you are well paid. And there are amenities available to employees, including a private country club in Lake Elmo equipped with four tennis courts, a club house and an 18-hole golf course.

The dedicated McKnight rose quickly in the firm, becoming president in 1929 and chairman in 1949. He died in 1978.

Another key to 3M's success is its sales force, one of the most dynamic in the country. Credit here belongs to the late Archibald G. Bush, who joined the firm in 1909 and worked there 57 years.

Bush was consumed by selling. His philosophy as simple: the first sale to a customer is important, but set a goal for the 100th sale.

The spirits of McKnight and Bush have been preserved by their successors in the board room and by 3M employees. The company continues to grow and prosper.

General Mills

In 1866, Cadwallader C. Washburn opened a small mill on the banks of the Mississippi River at St. Anthony Falls. It was a modest operation that Washburn never envisioned growing into General Mills, a multibillion-dollar corporation.

Winter wheat was popular during Washburn's time, but he figured he would make his mill a success using

Above: *Mickey's Diner in downtown St. Paul, a favorite of customers in jeans as well as those in tuxedoes and gowns.*

Facing page: *The IDS Tower (right) is the tallest building in downtown Minneapolis—for the present. At left is the Norwest Building.*
STEVE SCHNEIDER PHOTOS

spring wheat for flour. He was dismayed when his flour came out a sickly gray—not the white powder of winter wheat flour. But Washburn tinkered with his product until he got it white, and he sold it by saying it had better baking properties.

Washburn took on a partner, John Crosby, who ran the business side of the firm, by then called Washburn Crosby Co. Their flour won gold medals at the Millers International Exhibition in 1880. The partners decided to label their product Gold Medal Flour, and that has been a General Mills tag ever since.

In 1928, General Mills was created by a merger of Washburn Crosby and other milling companies. It became the largest flour milling company in the world within five months.

After World War II, General Mills executives were fascinated by the rapidly-increasing number of women taking jobs outside the home. There had to be a market involved. General Mills came up with instant hot cereals and convenience foods. And then almost-effortless-to-prepare cake mixes. The success of such foods was enormous.

For many years, General Mills lived off the likes of Wheaties and Cheerios and Bisquick, and, of course, Gold Medal Flour. Then, in the 1960s, the company decided to diversify. Besides producing consumer food, General Mills now is active in toys, fashion, specialty retailing and restaurants.

A unique management family is given credit for the success of General Mills. It began with James Stroud Bell who, in 1888, became president of Washburn Crosby. No one was better at merchandising flour at that time. He was followed by his son, James Ford Bell, a founder of General Mills, who ran the company from 1925 to 1947. Five years later, his son, Charles H. Bell, became president, holding that position until 1967.

All three Bells were highly competent executives who kept close track of business trends and who were not afraid to take a chance or two. Under their leadership, and those who followed them, General Mills grew into its multibillion-dollar status.

Dayton Hudson Corporation

George Draper Dayton didn't want to go into the dry goods business. He was a Worthington banker who owned an investment firm.

What Dayton wanted was to construct a six-story building at 7th Street and Nicollet Avenue in Minneapolis. He did that in 1901, when the location was at the edge of downtown.

Getting tenants was difficult. So, Dayton, to get one tenant, helped finance two young men in the dry goods business.

A year later, they literally had lost their shirts and Dayton found himself owning a dry goods store. He called it the Dayton Company.

All went well, however slowly, until a 1917 fire destroyed Dayton's shoe department. Dayton decided to build a new, bigger building at the same site.

Above: *Nicollet Mall in downtown Minneapolis was created for pedestrians—and buses and taxis.*

Facing page: *When the Minnesota Twins won the 1987 World Series, the Twin Cities exploded. Here is a celebration scene in St. Paul.*
STEVE SCHNEIDER PHOTOS

85

Above: *Twin Citians do just about everything on ice. Here is a St. Paul Winter Carnival softball game on the rocks.*

Facing page: *St. Paul and the Quadriga. St. Paul has experienced a renaissance in recent years.*
STEVE SCHNEIDER PHOTOS

George Dayton was a conservative, religious man. He would not open his store or advertise on Sunday because it was "God's day." He believed in a family business and brought his two sons, D. Draper Dayton and G. Nelson Dayton, into the firm.

The elder Dayton died in 1938 and G. Nelson Dayton became president.

But it took the elder's grandchildren to build the business into a giant operation. There were six of them: Donald, Bruce, Wallace, Kenneth, Douglas and George Dayton, active in management beginning after World War II.

Under their creative management, the company began building major shopping centers outside the city. First came Southdale in Edina, then Brookdale in Brooklyn Center, then Rosedale in Roseville, north of St. Paul, and then more. A huge acquisition was the Hudson Corporation of Detroit in 1969.

The brothers got into the discount business in 1962 by founding Target Stores and then branched into such things as book stores, hard goods retailing and jewelry stores.

The Daytons were innovative. In the 1960s for the first time in the area, a company went after the youth market: special teenage departments, a young look in advertising, promotions aimed at teenagers.

Dayton Hudson today, the eleventh largest retailing company in America, has sales of almost $10 billion and employs 126,000 people.

It's a good thing for the Twin Cities that those two young dry goods sellers didn't succeed.

St. Paul Companies

In 1853, four years after Minnesota became a territory, St. Paul Fire and Marine, now St. Paul Companies, was created in the river town east of the Mississippi.

A group of local businessmen were unhappy with the skimpy service provided St. Paul by east-coast insurance companies. What did they know or care about a faraway pioneer town?

So, more than 130 years ago, they formed their own, then called St. Paul Fire and Marine Insurance Co. It got a reputation, first in St. Paul, and then nationally as a reliable, honest, but creative firm.

The company was hit hard by the 1871 Great Chicago Fire and, in 1906, the San Francisco earthquake and fire. But it survived.

For many years, the firm was involved mainly in property-liability insurance, but, in the 1950s, it branched out: life, health, title and so on. Then came financial services.

But company executives never forgot that property-liability insurance was its big money maker. There was a major shakeup in the 1980s. Property-liability insurance was expanded. The other insurances and the financial services were sold. Added were wholesale brokerage, reinsurance and specialty lines.

Today it is represented by some 7,000 insurance agents throughout the world. It has assets of nearly $7 billion and annual revenues of about $3 billion.

CHAPTER
6

POLITICS
NO INSINUENDOS, PLEASE

Above: Parks are a big part of life in the Twin Cities. Here is a young swinger at play.

Right: The Twin Cities have most ambitious skyway systems. Small shops are located in parts of them. Here is one viewed over Marquette Avenue. STEVE SCHNEIDER PHOTOS

The Twin Cities long have been the center of Minnesota politics. The state has seen rural power diminish and the Cities' power grow. And the politics of Minnesota indicates the character of the region.

In *The Book of America,* by Neil R. Peirce and Jerry Hagstrom, there is the following:

"Search America from sea to sea and you will not find a state that has offered as close a model to the ideal of the successful society as Minnesota…The Minnesota political structure remains open, issue-oriented, responsive. Questioning how things are done—up to a very high level is not only tolerated but encouraged.

"Minnesota's greatest strength remained the clear focus of economic, political, and cultural leadership in her Twin Cities of Minneapolis and St. Paul"

So who were the politicians that made it all possible?

Floyd B. Olson

Had he lived longer, Floyd B. Olson, a Minneapolis native, might have become president of the United States.

As it was, he created a stir across the nation and was considered one of the most powerful and dynamic politicians of his time. He set the tone for those who followed him—a tradition of aggressive people who knew how to charm the populace.

When he died of pancreatic cancer in 1936, at age 45, he already had been Hennepin County Attorney and was elected to three terms as Minnesota's governor, beginning in office in January 1931.

The Twin Cities, of course, were directly affected by the politicians both state and local.

Olson was an impressive man: six-feet-two, a blue-eyed Scandinavian, virile, quick-witted and a man who could mix with people in a small-town saloon or in the salons of the White House.

The press, not at all friendly to him, often was forced to admit his power over people. The *Minneapolis Journal,* no longer in existence, once described an audience at an Olson speech:

"Those standing stood like statues from start to finish; those sitting sat forward on the edges of their chairs, intent not to miss a word."

Olson could create a well honed phrase. He once described the far left as people who yearn to "ride on a white horse with a pennant flying, hell bent for the barricades."

Known as a crusader for the underdog, Olson would anger many by appointing long-time arch conservatives to important jobs. An enemy legislature didn't bother him. He contended it just gave him more ammunition for his next political campaign.

Amidst all the oratory, Olson managed to get things done: a moratorium on farm foreclosures, relief appropriations, pension reform laws and Minnesota's first income tax.

A May Day celebration put on by Heart of the Beast Puppet Theater group in Minneapolis. STEVE SCHNEIDER

89

In his book, *The Political Career of Floyd B. Olson,* George H. Mayer characterizes the flamboyant governor:

"He attracted people from every walk of life, recalling their names and faces easily because the personalities behind them were really alive to him. He was gregarious to a fault, losing all sense of time in the pleasures of conversation and good fellowship. One day while political leaders paged him frantically in the hotels and restaurants of Brainerd, he sat in the kitchen of the Norwegian Lutheran Church, talking to the ladies and jotting down recipes for his wife. On another occasion, he left for the office at 8:45 a.m. to keep a crowded schedule of appointments, only to tarry for half an hour at the corner lot tossing a football with some children."

Harold Stassen

He has been called the creator of modern Minnesota Republican politics. It was Harold Stassen who, in the 1930s, decided Minnesota's Republican party should be less conservative, more moderate. And he made it that way.

Born poor in a Dakota County farmhouse, Stassen sold newspapers, and raised and sold skunks, rabbits and pigeons after school. In summer, he had a roadside vegetable stand.

The farm boy walked two miles to school and, at 14, graduated from high school.

He was a sharpshooter with a rifle and was a regular blue-ribbon winner at rural turkey shoots. After a stint as conductor on the St. Paul-Chicago run of a railroad, Stassen entered the University of Minnesota.

Still poor, he had to work his way through. He graduated at 19, went to law school and graduated there at 21. The tall, sandy-haired man began practicing law, but it was politics he really wanted.

Stassen's first elective office was as Dakota County Attorney. He served two terms and earned a reputation for hard work and courage.

During the 1932 milk strike, an agitator spoke before Dakota county farmers, telling them violence was the only answer. He yelled:

"Block the highways! Spill the milk! If the county attorney gets in your way, run him out!"

Stassen strolled up from the back of the room and said: "The county attorney is here." He said he would prosecute if there were any violence and then the politician in him emerged. He told them he would serve as their counsel free and try to get them higher milk prices.

At 31, Stassen decided it was time to be Minnesota's governor. He stumped the state—50,000 miles in total—and beat Elmer Benson, the Farmer-Labor incumbent by a quarter million votes. In 1938, he became the youngest governor in the United States and naturally received the tag: "Boy Wonder."

Two years later, the length then of the governor's term, Stassen was re-elected and that year he was floor manager for Wendell Willkie at the Republican National Convention. He was re-elected again in 1942, but resigned to enter the U. S. Navy.

In 1945, the "Boy Wonder" signed the United Nations charter as a member of the U.S. Delegation and later decided it was time to become president of the United States.

But he couldn't beat Thomas Dewey in 1948 for the Republican nomination and he became president of the University of Pennsylvania.

The rest of Stassen's political career has been *he runs, he loses*. In 1987, at age 80, he announced his intention to run for president for the eighth time.

But, despite his later failures, Stassen was most important to Minnesota. He was responsible, among other things, for reducing the state debt drastically, reorganizing governmental administration and, most importantly, for instituting comprehensive civil service. *The Book of America* describes the civil service impact:

"This fundamental reform has transformed the nature of Minnesota politics, making it a highly honorable profession in which citizens participate as willingly as in a United Fund drive or PTA; there simply are no "bosses," and virtually no one goes into Minnesota politics out of a patronage motive. Stassen made the government process in Minnesota a superior instrument of the people's will."

Hubert H. Humphrey

There was a lot of Floyd B. Olson in Hubert H. Humphrey. Both were men of the people, loved people and knew all the ways to captivate them.

Once, 25 couples who had been married for 50 years were invited by a dinner theater to celebrate their goldenwedding anniversaries. At intermission of the play, Humphrey showed up. He shook their hands and chatted with them until it was time for the show to resume.

A reporter, there to cover the anniversary, asked Humphrey: "Why did you come? There are only 50 people here." Replied the Minnesota senator:

"These people will not forget it. And they'll go home and tell all their friends and their friends will tell their friends and…"

Humphrey was born above his father's drug store in Wallace, South Dakota. His mother nicknamed him "Pinky" because of his reddish complexion. At Doland (South Dakota) High School, in 1927, Humphrey made a solemn announcement: he would one day be president of the United States. His teacher, Lulu Herther and the rest of the class, laughed. But Humphrey almost made it.

Above: *Noah Adams, who succeeded Garrison Keillor on Minnesota Public Radio, performs on the stage of St. Paul's World Theater.*

Facing page: *An interior of one of the newer downtown Minneapolis buildings: The Lincoln Centre. Major buildings in construction are the Norwest Bank building and an IBM structure.* STEVE SCHNEIDER PHOTOS

Above: *Volleyball games are common sights at Lake Calhoun and other beaches.*

Facing page: *A curse of spring for most Twin Citians is the dandelion. Here a patch grows freely not far from downtown Minneapolis.*
STEVE SCHNEIDER PHOTOS

He was as relentless as the light when it came to pursuit of political office. And he started a Democratic dynasty in Minnesota. Two of his most prominent proteges: Eugene McCarthy, who ran against Humphrey in 1968 for the Democratic nomination for president, and Walter Mondale.

The restless, energetic man left teaching political science at Macalester College in St. Paul to run for mayor of Minneapolis. The first time he lost. But, in 1945, he beat incumbent Marvin Kline.

The city was wide open. Prostitutes, gamblers, whatever. (Kline later was convicted of grand larceny in connection with a Sister Kenny Foundation scandal. He served three years of a 10-year prison sentence.)

New Mayor Humphrey had campaigned on a clean-up-the-city platform. He kept his promise—in a hurry.

He called in the police chief and told him to round up a squad of his toughest patrolmen. They were to "usher" the prostitutes, pimps and gamblers and other violators out of town. Put them on trains and buses. No arguments, no jailing, no crowding of court calendars. It worked.

While mayor, Humphrey and his political friends began discussing the members of a cabinet for President Humphrey.

In 1948, the Minneapolis mayor was elected to the U.S. Senate by 250,000 votes over his Republican opponent, Joseph Ball. That year, Humphrey had led the fight for a stronger civil rights bill at the Democratic National Convention—notwithstanding his "ushering" scheme.

In Washington, Humphrey ordered his staff to adhere to two fundamental rules:
- When voters wrote to complain about the government, always tell them the government is wrong.
- If someone comes to the office and wants to see "Pinky," give him or her royal treatment.

Humphrey made one admitted mistake as a junior senator: he put forth a bill in 1954 that would make membership in the Communist Party illegal. It was during the dark days of McCarthyism. The civil rights leader later apologized for it.

The Minnesota senator sought the Democratic nomination for vice president in 1956 and went up against John Kennedy for the Democratic nomination for president in 1960. He won the Wisconsin primary, but lost in West Virginia and it was all over.

In 1964, Lyndon Johnson chose Humphrey as his running mate and he became Vice President Humphrey. Always a liberal, Humphrey stubbornly supported the Johnson administration's policy in Vietnam and the rest of Southeast Asia.

It probably cost him the presidency in 1968.

As Author Larry Adcock reported: "He wept privately in despair every time he heard the student chant-of-the-day in 1968: 'Hubert Humphrey, LBJ, how many kids did you kill today?'"

In 1970, Humphrey successfully ran for the senate again and remained a Washington power until his death from cancer January 13, 1978. He was buried in Lakewood

Cemetery in Minneapolis. Author Adcock offers an anecdote that sums up Hubert H. Humphrey:

"One day in 1970, when, for once, the entire campaign schedule had been completed by 4:30 p.m., Humphrey and the veteran DFL campaigner D. J. Leary were headed back to the Twin Cities via helicopter. Leary looked forward to the first evening at home in a long while.

"But Humphrey spotted something on the ground. 'People!' he shouted. 'Voters! Set this thing down.' The pilot obeyed and set down in a field where the Gibbon, Minn., Rod & Gun Club—three men strong—were out shooting skeet. Humphrey took a turn and blasted three out of four skeet to smithereens.

"'This is Sibley County,' Leary complained. 'You can't find a Democrat anywhere in this county.'

"Humphrey replied: 'Listen, even Republicans know how to vote'."

Walter Mondale

Of all of Hubert Humphrey's proteges, Walter (Fritz) Mondale was the most successful politically. He, like Humphrey, became vice president of the United States and, like Humphrey, ran for president.

But he wasn't much like Humphrey.

As Geri Joseph, long a friend of Mondale, put it:

"Fritz will do things that put him in a controversial position, but he's not a daring person, he's not impulsive, he's not a risk-taker." Humphrey was all of those.

Mondale, born to poverty in southern Minnesota, was the son of Methodist minister Theodore Mondale. The family were fed from a small vegetable garden and produce from church-goers who couldn't afford to pay their minister.

The young Mondale had to work early in life. And the jobs weren't always pleasant: tying the legs of scalded chicken, inspecting pea plants for lice.

He managed to get to Macalester College in St. Paul and was intrigued with Humphrey. He volunteered to help get Humphrey reelected as Minneapolis mayor in 1947. And when Humphrey ran for the U.S. senate a year later, Mondale worked hard in rural southern Minnesota for his mentor.

At first, Mondale, without a car, hitchhiked the territory proclaiming the virtues of Humphrey. He decided to

try to con a car out of a Mankato dealer. Mondale described the scene, as recounted by Finlay Lewis of the *Minneapolis Star Tribune* in 1984:

"I'll never forget that—one of the most exciting days of my political career. Here I was, a deadbroke kid; I'd never seen any money, been hitchhiking, couldn't get any place I needed, dreamed all my life of having a car.

"My heart was in my throat. I figured he'd throw me outa there, trying to hustle him for a car. So he took me out back and there were all these cars.

"He swept his hand over the lot and said, 'OK, kid, pick any one you want. It's yours'."

After Macalester and a stint as an army corporal in the Korean War, Mondale went to the University of Minnesota Law School, graduating in 1956. Still fascinated by politics, he worked to get another Humphrey protege, Orville Freeman, elected Minnesota governor. (Freeman also later became Secretary of Agriculture in the Kennedy administration.)

Mondale's own entry into politics was by appointment: Freeman made him Minnesota Attorney General. His second political office also was by appointment: when Humphrey resigned his Senate seat to run for the vice presidency, Gov. Karl Rolvaag named Mondale to the vacated seat.

Unlike Humphrey, Mondale did not take Washington by storm. He moved slowly and studied the maneuvers of the more experienced senators. In 1968, he made his first major thrust. He got the Senate to pass a landmark open-housing bill that, without him would have died in committee.

In 1976, Jimmy Carter wanted a man from a northern state to be his running mate. He chose Mondale. And the Minnesotan became a most effective second-in-command at the White House.

When Carter, beset by problems including inflation and the Iran hostage crisis, was defeated for reelection in 1980, Mondale saw his chance to fulfill his dream of running for president. He sought and won the 1984 Democratic nomination for presidency.

Several things led to his defeat. His loyalty to Humphrey cost him politically. He would not attack the Vietnam war for fear it would embarrass his friend. He named a woman, Geraldine Ferraro, as his running mate and she turned out to be controversial. And he ran against incumbent Ronald Reagan, who was as popular as ice cream on a hot day.

Mondale now is back in Minneapolis practicing law.

Humphrey once gave his assessment of the man whom he had nurtured politically since the southern Minnesotan was a student:

"He was not a polarizer. Coupled all this with what was obvious talent. He was young, he was articulate, he was intelligent and clean-cut. He kept filling the bill. It's most amazing."

The Twin Cities Mayors

The mayors of Minneapolis and St. Paul are about alike as Groucho Marx and a Benedictine monk.

George Latimer, St. Paul's mayor, is flamboyant, talkative, jestful and humorous. Donald Fraser, of Minneapolis, is thoughtful, quiet, persistent and scholarly.

George Latimer

He spent his childhood in upstate New York and got a law degree from Columbia University. Joe DiMaggio is his hero and he readily lists his own faults:

"I wish I were smarter. I don't pay enough attention to details. I get bored fairly easily."

It was George Latimer's boredom with being a labor lawyer that pushed him into politics. He was a natural. Lori Sturdevant, of the *Minneapolis Star Tribune,* described Latimer's personality:

"He's winsome, he's funny. He fixes a brown-eyed gaze at people that says, "I care only about you and what you're saying." He draws energy from contact with people, and that energy seems to draw people to him in turn."

He drew enough people in 1976 to be elected mayor of St. Paul. And he's been in that office since.

Sporting a salt-and-pepper beard, Latimer is a compulsive worker. "If I'm doing two things at once, I tend to look for a third thing." He loves ceremonial functions: posing for a picture with a retiring policeman, signing autographs for high school students, going to churches to honor Eagle Scouts, cutting ribbons for the opening of new buildings.

He has not been without controversy. He publicly came out for a gay rights ordinance, supported a human sexuality course at the University of Minnesota while he was a regent and, despite strong neighborhood opposition, he advocated a Job Corps center at Bethel College.

The 51-year-old father of five preached the development of downtown St. Paul and got people to listen. Since he took office, there has been $750 million in downtown and related development. Said Latimer:"I've done a lot more than downtown development." He is credited with a housing rehabilitation project, beautifying the city with more trees and creating a home weather-proofing program.

Above: *In winter, industrial stacks in the Twin Cities seem to send out frozen smoke.*

Facing page: *A St. Paul scene that could be titled: Skyway with State Capitol.* STEVE SCHNEIDER PHOTOS

Quipped the mayor: "I don't want to be guilty of modesty."

In 1986, Latimer, a Democrat, ran for governor against the incumbent, Rudy Perpich, also a Democrat. Latimer lost, and went back to running St. Paul.

The mayor, who lists Mark Twain as his favorite author, once characterized his style of political operation:

"The fact is, nobody in this city gets around as much as I do. They [the press] can write their annual story about how many trips I take to Washington, the council can get crotchety and call me an emperor and a king, but the fact is, the people know I'm the guy who gets out there when they want me."

Donald Fraser

The Minneapolis mayor once contended that nobody would believe him if "they heard me tell a really funny joke." That is not necessarily so, but it snugly fits his image.

Donald Fraser, 63, is a hard-working, determined leader who calls Thomas Jefferson his personal hero. The Minneapolis native has had a long political career, but lists being Minneapolis mayor as "the best time in my life."

He graduated cum laude from the University of Minnesota, majoring in mathematics. He went on to get his law degree at the university in 1944. His father, Everett Fraser, was law school dean at the time.

Fraser worked to get Hubert Humphrey elected to the Senate in 1948 and became a friend of Walter Mondale. Those associations led him into politics.

In 1954, the man who reads historical fiction was elected to his first political position: member of the Minnesota State Senate. His work there included sponsoring legislation for reforms in education, welfare, taxation and civil rights.

He was chairman of Minnesota Citizens for Kennedy in 1960. It was time to go to Washington and, in 1962, he ran for the House of Representatives and won by about 7,000 votes. The liberal Democrat with the conservative lifestyle spent eight terms in the House.

In 1978, he tried for the U.S. Senate, but lost. The quiet man came back to Minneapolis and successfully ran for mayor in 1981. He celebrated his victory with a smile and a bottle of pop.

Fraser—who admits he cannot remember names but his wife, Arvonne, can—considers the following his major accomplishments as mayor: getting politics out of the police department and working on structural improvements in city government, including cooperation between the mayor and the city council.

In Congress, he wants to be remembered for laying a legislative basis for bringing human rights into U.S. foreign policy. In 1985, he received the Minnesota International Human Rights award from the Minnesota Lawyers International Human Rights Committee. The speaker at the presentation was Harlan Cleveland, director of the University of Minnesota Humphrey Institute of Public Affairs. In part, Cleveland said of Fraser:

"As a result of legislation he authored, powerful searchlights now shine in dark corners of authority around the world"and human rights must now be part of each year's judgments about economic and military aid...

"What his visitors find, as we his neighbors know, is a man of astonishing modesty, surprisingly approachable, more deeply than ever concerned for the fate of the individual in the jostling of big organizations, and for the human race in a world overstuffed with nuclear weapons. He is a creative and steadfast friend of the inherent dignity of human beings."

All that about a man who says if he has learned one thing in life it's "not to take myself too seriously."

The Maverick Mayors

Minneapolis and St. Paul have had mayors who make the description "colorful" legitimate.

Both had the first name Charles. One was a real cop who didn't want to be and the other was a fantasy cop who loved it.

Charles McCarty

They called him "Super Mayor" and he drove a 1970 black Lincoln Continental dubbed "Super Car."

Charles McCarty, St. Paul's mayor in the early 1970s, had a yen to be a policeman most of his life. He drove "Super Car" at night and chased law-breaking motorists.

"Super Car" was equipped with a siren and flashing red lights—and a device that would turn red traffic lights green.

The idea was that, when McCarty was in full pursuit of a motorist, he wouldn't be bothered by traffic signals.

On December 19, 1971, he observed a traffic violator and gave chase. He did not turn on the siren and flashing red lights, and the red-light-green gadget didn't work. Mc-

Minneapolis and St. Paul have had mayors who make the description "colorful" legitimate.

Opposite page: Town Square Park, St. Paul. STEVE SCHNEIDER

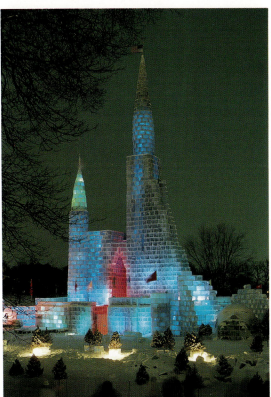

Clockwise from upper left:
An example of snow sculpture on Harriet Island—an art competition of the Winter Carnival.
The Ice Dragon, in Rice Park, is a favorite of children at the Winter Carnival.
Many hours of work and much skill go into the ice sculptures at Rice Park.
The Ice Palace, under construction, before it is transformed into a thing of beauty.
The St. Paul Winter Carnival Ice Palace, a nationally renowned project visited by thousands.

Facing page: It's called the St. Paul Athletic Club toss, part of the St. Paul Winter Carnival.
STEVE SCHNEIDER PHOTOS

Above: *A passenger plane descends for the Minneapolis–St. Paul International Airport.*
Right: *A jogger makes his way around Lake of the Isles in Minneapolis.*

Facing page, left: *Northrup Auditorium, University of Minnesota.*
Right: *At the Minneapolis Zoo.*
STEVE SCHNEIDER PHOTOS

Carty went through a red light and crashed into a car at the intersection. The violator got away and "Super Car" suffered damage.

Commented *Minneapolis Tribune Columnist* Don Morrison:

"So, we may charitably say the mayor himself was a victim. He trusted a gadget, which always is bad policy. In a larger sense, I suppose, he also is a victim of his own publicity.

"The media have tended to feed McCarty's flamboyant self-image. Much of the reporting of his council tantrums and extra-curricular antics, to be sure, has been in the tone of wry amusement, as one tolerantly regards a bad-boy nephew."

Charles Stenvig

Charles Stenvig, a Minneapolis burglary detective, didn't want to be a policemen. In 1956, he took the police examination "for kicks." He already had been offered a job by the Morton Salt Co.

"I wish I had taken the Morton job," he said years later.

One of his first jobs on the force was directing traffic at one of the busiest intersections in downtown Minneapolis.

"It almost drove me out of my mind," he said. "I don't think I took a drink of hard liquor before that. Those old ladies—you try to save them and they cuss you out."

Stenvig, who played the drums for relaxation, was considered impulsive, erratic and rash by his opponents. But he was elected to three terms as mayor of Minneapolis.

The conservative mayor had problems with the language.

"I was terrible in English in school," he said. "My 'dese' and 'dems' still show up."

His most famous utterance was after a setback in his political career. He said that he could hardly be expected to win when the local newspapers kept "hurling insinuendos" at him.

100

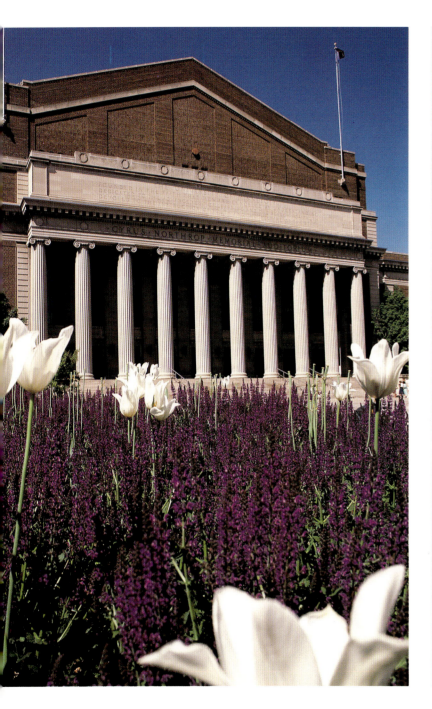
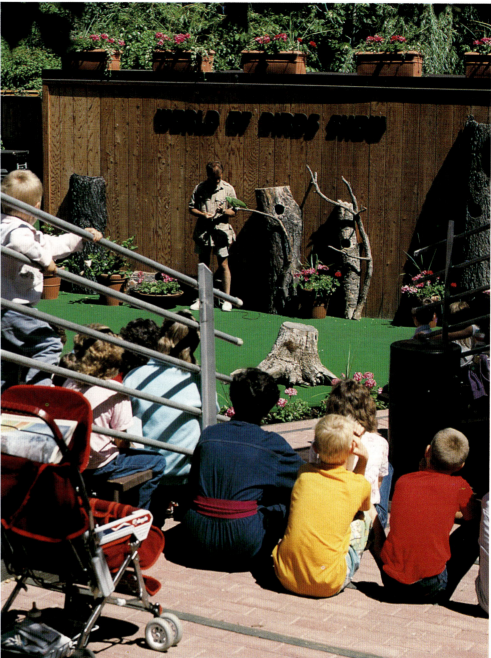

For Further Reading

Atwater, Isaac. *History of the City of Minneapolis*. Munsell, 1893.

Berman, Lael. *Landmarks—Old and New: Minneapolis and St. Paul and Surrounding Areas*. Minneapolis: Nodin Press, 1988.

Cross, Marion. *Pioneer Harvest*. Minneapolis: Farmers and Mechanics Savings Bank, 1849.

Borchert, John R., and Neil C. Gustafson. *Atlas of Minnesota Resources & Settlement*. Minneapolis: Center for Urban and Regional Affairs, 1980.

Gray, James. *University of Minnesota: 1851-1951*. Minneapolis: University of Minnesota Press, 1951.

Grossman, Mary Ann and Tom Thomsen, eds. *Minnesota Almanac*. Taylors Falls, Min.: John R. Brekke, 1987.

Guest Informant 50 Years: Minneapolis/St. Paul. Woodland Hills, Calif.: Guest Informant, 1987.

Hess, Jeffrey A. *Their Splendid Legacy: The First 100 Years of the Minneapolis Society of Fine Arts*. Minneapolis Society of Fine Arts, 1985.

Historic St. Paul Buildings. St. Paul City Planning Board, 1964.

Kane, Lucile M. *The Waterfall that Built a City*. St. Paul: Minnesota Historical Society, 1966.

Kunz, Virginia Brainard. *St. Paul: Saga of an American City*. Woodland Hills, Calif.: Windsor Publications, 1977.

Kunz, Virginia Brainard. *St. Paul: A Modern Renaissance*. Northridge, Calif.: Windsor Publications, Inc., 9186.

Kunz, Virginia Brainard. *Minnetonka Yacht Club Centennial: 1872-1972*. Minnetonka Sailing School: 1972.

Mayer, George H. *The Political Career of Floyd B. Olson*. St. Paul: Minnesota Historical Society Press, 1987.

Mohr, Howard. *How to Talk Minnesotan*. New York: Penguin Books, 1987.

1988 Minnesota Weatherguide Calendar. Freshwater Society, the Science Museum of Minnesota and WCCO Weather Center, 1987.

Ouchi, William. *The M-Form Society*. Reading, Maine: Addison-Wesley, 1984.

Peirce, Neal R., and Jerry Hagstrom. *The Book of America: Inside 50 States Today*. New York: W.W. Norton & Co., 1983.

Stepanovich, Joseph. *City of Lakes: An Illustrated History of Minneapolis*. Woodland Hills, Calif.: Windsor Publications, 1982.

Theatre Profiles. New York: Theatre Communications Group, Inc., 1973.

Trenerry, Walter N. *Murder in Minnesota: A Collection of True Cases*. St. Paul: Minnesota Historical Society, 1962.

Williams, J. Fletcher. *A History of the City of St. Paul to 1875*. St. Paul: Minnesota Historical Society Press, 1983.

Facing page: *Downtown St. Paul is reflected in the waters of the Mississippi River.* STEVE SCHNEIDER

AMERICAN GEOGRAPHIC PUBLISHING

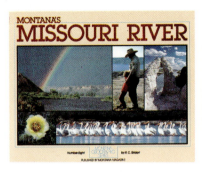 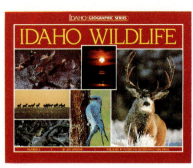 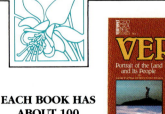 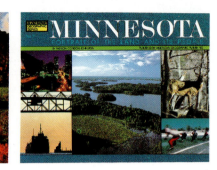

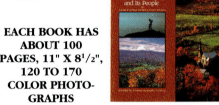

EACH BOOK HAS ABOUT 100 PAGES, 11" X 8½", 120 TO 170 COLOR PHOTOGRAPHS

Enjoy, See, Understand America State by State

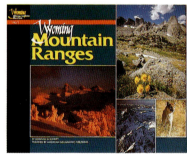

American Geographic Publishing Geographic Series of the States

Lively, colorful, beautifully illustrated books specially written for these series explain land form, animals and plants, economy, lifestyle and history of each state or feature. Generous color photography brings each state to life and makes each book a treat to turn to frequently. The geographic series format is designed to give you more information than coffee-table photo books, yet so much more color photography than simple guide books.

Each book includes:
- Colorful maps
- Valuable descriptions and charts of features such as volcanoes and glaciers
- Up-to-date understanding of environmental problems where man and nature are in conflict
- References for additional reading, agencies and offices to contact for more information
- Special sections portraying people in their homes, at work, in the countryside

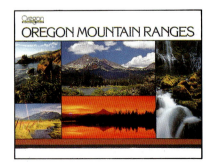 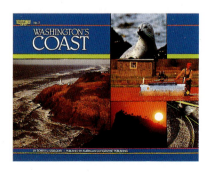

for more information write:
**American Geographic Publishing
P.O. Box 5630
Helena, Montana 59604**